HANNAH'S SONG

HANNAH'S SONG

What love looks like

Diana Hagee

JHM
PUBLISHING

ISBN: 978-1-61795-864-9

Printed in the United States of America
17 18 19 20 21 VPI 8 7 6 5 4 3 2 1

I dedicate this book to my nine granddaughters—
Mckenzie, Kassidee, Micah, Hannah, Victoria,
Olivia, Elliana, Caroline, and Madison.
May you all be surrounded by the Lord's goodness,
mercy, and supernatural favor,
and may your character reflect
the qualities of a Godly woman,
for your lives are destined for greatness!

Contents

Acknowledgments ✎ 9

1. The Heart of the Matter ✎ 11

2. Biblical Backdrop ✎ 17

3. Sanctified—The Beauty of Holiness ✎ 25
1 Samuel 1:1–5

4. Sorrow—My Sadness for His Joy ✎ 37
1 Samuel 1:6–9, 14–16

5. Supplication—The Silent Cry ✎ 63
1 Samuel 1:9–13, 17–18

6. Sacrifice—Absolute Submission ✎ 95
1 Samuel 1:19–28

7. The Song—The Power of Praise ✎ 115
1 Samuel 2:1–10

8. Supernatural Favor—Abiding in His Blessings ✎ 141
1 Samuel 2:11, 18–36

9. Significance—Destined for Greatness ✎ 167
1 Samuel 3:1–4, 10, 19–21; 10:1; 16:13

10. The New Song ✎ 185

Notes ✎ 191

Journal Notes ✎ 198

Acknowledgments

Thanks to my husband and constant encourager.

Thanks to my son,
who urged me to write a study on Hannah.

Thanks to Jo-Ann and Kris,
who helped make this journey possible.

Thanks to Hannah, who set a standard
of righteousness for all women.

And thanks always to the Lord,
who is so faithful to show the way.

Chapter 1

The Heart of the Matter

*For no other foundation can anyone lay
than that which is laid, which is Jesus Christ.*

1 Corinthians 3:11

Several years ago I wrote a book entitled *Ruth: The Romance of Redemption*, in which I confessed my apprehension about studying and teaching the Word of God.

For years the Word of God intimidated me. I was afraid to open its pages for fear I would not understand its message. As a pastor's wife I knew I would be expected to interpret the words of this sacred Book to others, and the weight of this mandate was too heavy to carry. I was overwhelmed. What if I made a mistake? What if I led people astray? It was a risk I could not take. So I did nothing.

Slowly, at the prodding of my ever-thoughtful husband, I began to examine the Word for answers to my questions. I searched its infinite wisdom for direction. I combed its pages for comfort, and as time passed, the Word became a great and inseparable friend.

The first books of the Bible I studied were Ruth and Esther. I chose them for two reasons: First, they were short, and I felt secure in that. Second, they were about women. At the time, this question amazed me: Why would the God who created the universe and formed man with His own hands dedicate entire books of His consecrated Word to women?

I have now been a pastor's wife for forty years, and what an insightful journey it has been! I've realized Scripture's high regard for women and appreciated the important roles and assignments with which God has entrusted us. Yet no matter how often I open the pages of the Bible, my prayer is still the same: "Teach me, Father, to hear from Your precious Word. Be patient with me, for I know so little. Show me what You would have me learn from Your sacred Scripture."[1]

The Lord has been ever faithful. He has always heard my prayer and He has always answered. I have led numerous Bible studies in the past several years, and now, at the encouragement of our son, Pastor Matthew, I will share some of the biblical truths that have encouraged me and the women at Cornerstone Church.

ABOUT THIS STUDY

One of the great advantages of living with a pastor is the personal license to ask for his insights when studying Scripture. Pastor Hagee has always said that before one can fully understand the Bible, the following questions, known as the six *W*s, must be answered:

- *When* was the book written?
- *To whom* was it written?
- *Why* was it written?
- *What* was the theme of the writing?
- *Where* did the narrative take place?
- *Who* are the major players in the story?

What I have learned from this practice is that context and application are imperative to understanding God's message to His people through His Word.

Another advantage to being a pastor's wife is getting to know the extraordinary people who cross our path. Many days I have sat as a silent witness, listening to distinguished men of God discuss Scripture. I remember one particular conversation that my husband had with Derek Prince, his beloved mentor and a celebrated Bible scholar. Their discussion was focused on God's purpose for Scripture. This exchange can best be summarized in Derek's book *Foundational Truths for Christian Living*, where he described the basic themes of the Bible.

The Old Testament chronicles creation. It reveals God's character and His dealings with individuals and with nations. It records the fall of man and those consequences, the history of the descendants of Adam and Eve, and the details of God's dealings with Abraham and his lineage. Included in this revelation are God's laws, His justice, His judgments, His mercy, and His faithfulness to keep the covenants and promises He made, whether with individuals or with nations—especially when dealing with Israel. One such promise to Israel was that God would send a Redeemer that would deliver them from the sin of disobedience and restore them to His grace, mercy, and favor eternally. The New Testament documents the fulfillment of this promise in the Person of Jesus, the Christ whose title is derived from a Greek word, *Christos*, which means "Messiah" or "Anointed One" in Hebrew. Jesus satisfied everything that the Old Testament foretold about His coming. Ultimately, "the Old Testament and the New Testament are linked together to form a single, harmonious revelation of God and His purposes for man."[2]

With this insightful synopsis of Scripture as our foundation, we can now begin our Bible study series. These studies are compiled from the teachings that are presented in the Cornerstone Church Naomi-Ruth Discipleship Class.

FOURFOLD PURPOSE

The purpose of this study is fourfold. It is intended to:

1. Help lay a foundation of Bible knowledge;
2. Offer the opportunity to search the Word for answers to everyday life;
3. Provide insight into the meaning of the Scriptures; and
4. Equip the reader to live the victorious, committed life of a believer.

The New King James Version of the Bible is referenced in this study unless otherwise noted. I will use the full name of the book in Scripture, followed by the chapter and verse—for example, Deuteronomy 12:1–14 refers to the book of Deuteronomy, chapter 12, verses 1 through 14.

Our study begins with a biblical backdrop. This historical overview answers the six *W*s just mentioned, which will assist us in understanding the setting of the story and the facts about the central characters. Once the backdrop is set, the lessons will encompass six main sections:

- The first is "Scriptural Foundations," which identifies and expounds on the specific verses selected for study.
- The next section is "Life Application," which gives you the opportunity for interactive participation.
- The third section features "Life Stories." These personal testimonies are chosen to help you relate to the themes of the lesson.
- The fourth section is entitled "Spiritual Checklist." This is a vital portion of our study. Pastor Hagee teaches that "God cannot change what we will not confront." It is meant to provide a private time of self-examination—a moment of intimate interaction between you and the Holy Spirit. This time of personal reflection will help confirm you are on the right path to your divine destiny.
- The fifth section is titled "Step of Faith." When Jesus Christ performed miracles, He required the recipients to take a step of faith. My prayer is that each study will move you to take positive action that will bring the change you may need in your life. Remember this truth: the most important step of faith is the *first* step.
- The final section is titled "Proclamation." A scriptural proclamation announces in an official manner what the Word of God declares. We must take ownership of the Lord's written promises; we should verbalize them and release His power over our lives.

The most important step of faith is the first step.

In order for this Bible study to be effective, it is vitally important to do the following:

1. Begin each lesson with prayer.

2. Set aside a specific time to be with the Lord. Time is among your most precious possessions. Give Him a portion of it, and He will reward you.

3. Your Bible will be your loyal companion—don't hesitate to write in the margins of its pages. I find that including the date in my notes often helps me better reflect on my journey with the Lord.

4. Carefully read all scriptural references provided. To fully understand their meaning may require reading them more than once, and possibly in different versions of the Bible.

5. Read each question thoroughly. When you're offering a scriptural answer, make sure you include the Bible reference (the book, chapter, and verse) in the space provided. This will not only help you refer to it later but allow you to adequately support your position when communicating it to others. Feel free to use the "Journal Notes" section provided in the back of this study if you need more space.

6. Answer the "Scriptural Checklist" questions truthfully. You will find it liberating to honestly journal your innermost feelings. This is part of your intimate time with God.

7. Make sure that whatever you list in the "Step of Faith" is personally achievable. Be realistic, and know that the Lord is your Champion—He wants you to succeed!

Chapter 2

Biblical Backdrop

Show me Your ways, O LORD; teach me Your paths.
Lead me in Your truth and teach me,
for You are the God of my salvation;
on You I wait all the day.
PSALM 25:4-5

We begin our study by providing answers to the six *W*s in the story of Hannah, which was authored by her son, Samuel the prophet, as recorded in 1 Samuel.

When *was 1 Samuel written?*
Originally, 1 and 2 Samuel were one manuscript. They remained this way until the fourteenth century.[1] In the Hebrew writings, 1 Samuel immediately followed the book of Judges.[2] It is important

to note that the last verse in Judges describes the condition of the times: "In those days there was no king in Israel; everyone did what was right in his own eyes" (Judges 21:25). "Those days" refers to the time in history when Israel was far from God.

The book of Judges records a dark era in Israel's history in which the Israelites were often ruled by their carnal nature rather than the law of God. As a direct result of their disobedience, they suffered hostile oppression. The Lord was Israel's King, and He ever mercifully sent judges—leaders like Deborah, Gideon, and Samuel—to represent Him and to set the Israelites back on the right path. Yet time and again Israel would rebel, and time and again God was faithful to send another deliverer because of His covenant promises to Abraham, Isaac, and Jacob.

Ultimately, the people demanded a mortal king to rule over them like other nations (1 Samuel 8:5). 1 Samuel details the history of Israel from the end of the age of Judges to the death of Saul, Israel's first appointed king. These two events cover almost 110 years, placing the timeline of the book from about 1120 to 1010 BC.[3]

To whom *was the book of Samuel written?*

1 Samuel was written to the Israelites, providing them a historical account of the rise of two kings, Saul and David, during the time of the prophet Samuel.

Why *was the story of Hannah written?*

Hannah's story was memorialized to emphasize the power of prayer, faith, and praise. While the people demanded a king, Hannah cried out to God for a son, and it was God's divine plan to establish the throne of Israel on a woman's prayer.[4]

What *are the themes of the story?*

The major focuses of 1 Samuel are an accounting of the last days of the Judges, the history of Samuel's life, the rise and fall of King Saul, and the ascent of David. In between these storylines are the interlaced themes of obedience, sacrifice, prayer, faith, and praise.

Where *did the story of Hannah take place?*

Hannah lived in Ramathaim Zophim (1 Samuel 1:1), located in the hill country of Ephraim. The other setting for the story is fourteen miles north, in the city of Shiloh.

Shiloh is derived from the Hebrew word, *She-lo*, meaning "He Who Is."[5] Joshua established the tabernacle of meeting with its sacred contents (the ark of the covenant) in Shiloh after moving it from Gilgal. The ark of the covenant is a chest containing the two stone tablets inscribed with the Ten Commandments. God commanded Moses to make the ark while the Jews were camped at Sinai (Exodus 25:10–22; 37:1–9). It was constructed and carried by the Israelites in their desert wanderings after the exodus from Egypt. The ark was the most sacred object in the tabernacle of meeting and eventually in Jerusalem until the destruction of the first temple in 586 BC. It was housed and used for religious service in the Holy of Holies—a sacred area that only the High Priest was allowed to enter.

As the only physical manifestation of God on earth, the ark of the covenant was the most important symbol of the Jewish faith. It is significant that Judaism focuses on man's actions and beliefs while rejecting any physical manifestations of worship. The worship of graven images, exemplified by the construction of the golden calf of Exodus 32, is harshly condemned throughout the Torah. The ark of the covenant is the one exception. The traditions associated with the ark and the severe penalties God assigned to anyone who misused it confirm its significance to the Jewish faith.[6]

> Now the whole congregation of the children of Israel assembled together at Shiloh, and set up the tabernacle of meeting there. (Joshua 18:1)

> Let us bring the ark of the covenant of the LORD from Shiloh to us, that when it comes among us it may save us from the hand of our enemies. (1 Samuel 4:3)

Who *are the major characters in the study?*

Even though the principal characters in 1 Samuel are Samuel, Saul, and David, we will base our study on those individuals directly involved in Hannah's life:

- *Elkanah* (1 Samuel 1:1)—Hannah's husband. His name means "God Is Owner."[7] He was the nineteenth direct descendant from the patriarch Jacob through the tribe of Levi (1 Chronicles 6:22–33), and he was a prophet in Israel.

- *Peninnah* (1 Samuel 1:1)—Elkanah's second wife. Her name means "Red Pearl."[8] Known as Hannah's adversary, Peninnah had the blessing of many children but the sorrow of being loved less by her husband.

- *Hophni and Phinehas* (1 Samuel 1:3)—The sons of Eli, the High Priest. Hophni means "Pugilist" (combatant or rebel); Phinehas means "Serpent's Mouth."[9] Though Eli's sons were priests in the tabernacle, they were immoral men who did not honor the Lord or His law (1 Samuel 2:12).

- *Eli* (1 Samuel 1:9)—High Priest and judge of Israel. His name means "My God."[10] He was the only man in the early days of Israel's history to hold these two offices.

  Shiloh was the center of religious life for the people of Israel, and it was where the tabernacle of meeting stood. Eli was the High Priest of Shiloh and the fourth in line of the unbroken chain of Oral Law, beginning with Moses and continuing through Joshua and Phinehas. It is not clear why Eli succeeded in the office of High Priest and not Phinehas's son.[11]

  Eli became judge at the age of fifty-eight, after the death of Samson, and held his positions for forty years, until his tragic death at the age of ninety-eight.[12] The Lord allowed Eli to disciple Samuel even though he failed miserably to train his own sons.

- *Samuel* (1 Samuel 1:19)—Hannah and Elkanah's eldest son. His name means "Heard of God."[13] As a result of his mother's vow, Samuel grew up in the tabernacle of God and was trained by Eli, the High Priest of Shiloh, in temple service.

  Samuel became the last of the judges (1 Samuel 7:15) and was established as a prophet to the nation of Israel (1 Samuel 3:20). The sovereign God prepared Samuel from a very young age to lead God's people back to righteousness. Samuel wrote the books of Judges and Ruth, as well as those bearing his name; the latter were completed by the records of Nathan and Gad after Samuel's death.[14]

- *Hannah* (1 Samuel 1:2)—The favored wife of Elkanah. Her name means "Beauty."[15] We do not know what Hannah's outward appearance was like, but the meaning of her name revealed her true inner spirit and grace. Hannah is among several women in Scripture who cried out to God for children. The others include Abraham's wife, Sarah (Genesis 15–21); Isaac's wife, Rebekah (Genesis 25:21); Jacob's wife Rachel (Genesis 29–30); and Elizabeth, the cousin of Jesus's mother, Mary (Luke 1).

Hannah, who was barren for many years, endured heartache, frustration, and a deep feeling of inadequacy in a culture that honored motherhood. She faced daily ridicule from her spiteful counterpart, the prolific Peninnah, and even beyond the walls of her tent, she could not elude the humiliation associated with a barren woman in her culture. Still, Hannah was a woman of patience, perseverance, and courage who chose to pray at the doorpost of the tabernacle of the Lord. Hannah cried out to God with absolute faith that He would hear her petition and answer it.

Hannah's answered prayer was named Samuel. He became the prophet whom God called to anoint Saul, the king chosen by the people; and David, the son of Jesse, the first king of Israel chosen by God.

It was God's divine plan to establish the throne of Israel on a woman's prayer.

What did you learn from the six Ws?

_____

_____

_____

_____

_____

_____

_____

*What did you learn from the meaning of the principal characters'
names?*

_____

_____

_____

_____

_____

_____

_____

Chapter 3

Sanctified— The Beauty of Holiness

Give to the LORD the glory due His name;
bring an offering, and come before Him.
Oh, worship the LORD in the beauty of holiness!
1 CHRONICLES 16:29

SCRIPTURAL FOUNDATION

Read 1 Samuel 1:1–5.

Now there was a certain man of Ramathaim Zophim, of the mountains of Ephraim, and his name was Elkanah the son of Jeroham, the son of Elihu, the son of Tohu, the son of Zuph, an Ephraimite. And

he had two wives: the name of one was Hannah, and the name of the
other Peninnah. Peninnah had children, but Hannah had no children.
This man went up from his city yearly to worship and sacrifice to the
LORD of hosts in Shiloh. Also the two sons of Eli, Hophni and Phinehas,
the priests of the LORD, were there. And whenever the time came for
Elkanah to make an offering, he would give portions to Peninnah his
wife and to all her sons and daughters. But to Hannah he would give
a double portion, for he loved Hannah, although the LORD had closed
her womb.

Elkanah was a righteous man living in a religiously corrupt time in Israel's history. The name of his village, Ramathaim Zophim, means "Two High Places of the Watchmen," which referred to the watchmen (prophets) who occupied two towers and kept a constant vigil over the land. This is also an apt description of Elkanah's character: he was a prophetic watchman for his people.

The Hebrew derivative of Ramathaim has the numerical value of two hundred, and Zophim translates to the word *prophets*. Hebrew scholars therefore conclude that Elkanah was one of two hundred prophets who prophesied in his time. He was not only a prophet; he was a Kohathite, who were among the most import- ant in the Levitical tribes (1 Chronicles 6:33–34).[1] Being a Levite, he faithfully kept Jewish law, which called for the Israelites to go to the tabernacle of meeting in Shiloh three times a year to cele- brate the Festival of Unleavened Bread (Passover), the Festival of the Harvest (Pentecost), and the Festival of Shelters (Tabernacles) (Exodus 34:23; Deuteronomy 16:16).

The opening scenes of 1 Samuel depict the devout Elkanah taking his family to worship in Shiloh in obedience to God's mandate. Hannah was favored by Elkanah; such regard would not have existed if she were not a noble woman who led a holy life submitted to God and her husband. While at Shiloh, Hannah would go to the tabernacle of meeting and offer her sacred petition to the Lord. To do this, she had to be pure of heart, spirit, and mind.

LIFE APPLICATION

Pursue peace with all people, and holiness,
without which no one will see the Lord.
HEBREWS 12:14

I'm sure Hannah was distressed by Peninnah's constant boasting about her quiver full of children. The barren Hannah could easily have felt justified in angrily repaying evil for evil, especially when she was the favored wife of her husband, but she chose to do right in the sight of God and "pursue peace." Hannah elected to set herself apart—she had an appointment with God—and prepared to approach the tabernacle of meeting, holy before the Lord.

> *We cannot enter into the presence*
> *of our Father in heaven without holiness.*

Just as Hannah could not pray at the tabernacle without holiness, we cannot enter into the presence of our Father in heaven without holiness. We must remember that the ultimate purpose of our salvation is to be in the presence of God now and for eternity.

Read Psalm 24:3–5 and Matthew 5:8. List the traits of those who qualify to stand in the presence of God.

_____

_____

_____

_____

Through His death and resurrection, Jesus intended to develop His kindred spirit in us, transforming us to His nature. The more we pursue peace and purity of heart and mind, the more we are like Him; and the more we are like Him, the more we become holy (sanctified). Holiness—being sacredly set apart—is the character of God. It is the nature of His being.[2]

Read Psalm 1:1–3; Ephesians 4:22–24; 1 Peter 1:13–15. What do these scriptures caution us to avoid and encourage us to pursue?

_____

_____

_____

_____

_____

_____

We are human—God is not! God's nature is holy—ours is not! He is the embodiment of purity—we are not! This separation can only be bridged by God Himself.[3] The Bridge the Father has put in place that brings us into His presence is Jesus Christ—He is the connection. He is the Way.

Read Isaiah 35:8–10 and John 14:6. What do these verses say about the walk of holiness?

_____

_____

_____

_____

_____

_____

_____

_____

_____

As women of God, we must walk the "way of holiness" by heeding God's voice through His Word and obeying His mandates. The rule of thumb is this: if you have to pray about something being right in His sight, it usually isn't.

Search the Scriptures for at least five verses that speak of God's holiness and write them down.

....

....

....

....

....

> *If you have to pray about something being right in His sight, it usually isn't.*

Christ's victory over Satan happened at the cross, where Jesus willingly laid down His life and submitted to God, His Father. It was an act of ultimate obedience; it was where our sins were atoned for through the shed blood of our Savior; it was where the enemies of Divine Authority were defeated.

Jesus set Himself apart from the presence of sin and walked in humility, allowing the Holy Spirit to be His guide. He set Himself apart with absolute righteousness and goodness. Our lives can also be set apart if we follow Christ's example. We are to be holy as Christ is holy. Therefore, when we approach God's throne, we too—like Hannah—must be set apart from the presence of sin and its consequences. However, this cannot be accomplished without Jesus, who at the cross took our sins away and gave us His righteousness.

Read Psalm 4:3. What does this verse say about being set apart?

When God makes a promise, there is usually a condition associated with that promise. God vowed to dwell among us and be our God, but first we must set ourselves apart from anything that would separate us from Christ our Savior.

What promises does the Lord make to His people in 2 Corinthians 6:16–18?

Read 2 Corinthians 6:14 and 7:1. Record what these verses are saying and what they mean to you.

LIFE STORIES

Not all of us can do great things.
But we can do small things with great love.
MOTHER TERESA

After raising her two children, Agnes Havlis made the decision in 1974 to resume her career as a social worker. With the blessing of her husband, she began to volunteer with a Christian counseling service. Recognizing Agnes's intense passion for at-risk children, the director of the center asked if she would consider starting an adoption agency. To Agnes, the request was overwhelming because of her inexperience with the adoption process. Yet she had lost her mother and father at an early age, and she knew the heartache of growing up without one's parents. So Agnes answered the call.

Working countless hours a week without pay, Agnes helped open the doors to Hope Services of Burden Bearers. The center assisted teenaged girls during their pregnancies and placed their children in loving homes.

The door of hope was opened wider with the fall of the Romanian dictatorship in 1989. The world media broadcasted news and pictures of the war-torn country's neglected and abused orphans, and Agnes immediately knew she had to take action to help them.

Thanks to Agnes's determination and tireless perseverance, the government miraculously agreed to let Hope Services place Romania's orphans into American families. As the agency expanded its work into China and Russia, Agnes rejoiced with every parent who welcomed a newly adopted child, and she shed tears of anguish when governments in other countries said no.

Thirty-one years after Agnes set herself apart for her divine calling, she made this statement: "Adoption helps just a small fraction of those who are abandoned . . . but every child you're able to help is invaluable, absolutely invaluable." Agnes Havlis stayed true to her personal pledge: "To extend Christ's love by providing solutions that best meet a child's need for a safe, stable and nurturing home."[4]

༄

Mother Teresa once said, "Love cannot remain by itself—it has no meaning. Love has to be put into action, and that action is service." We may not all be like Mother Teresa, or even Agnes Havlis, yet we can all say yes to God when He calls. We can all show the unconditional love of the Lord to those around us. We can all strive to be more like Christ by adopting His nature. We can all set ourselves apart for service in the kingdom of God. We can all take action, whether through intercession, ministry to the aged or infirmed, or by lovingly serving our own families. It is through our action and service that we show what love looks like.

However we choose to fulfill our service, it should always be done for the glory of God, with a pure and loving heart, and with the intent to shine the light of the gospel in an otherwise dark world. Once we are set apart *from* the world and set apart *to* God, we can:

- *Hear His voice* (Read Deuteronomy 28:1; Job 37:2–5; John 10:27–28.)

- *Obey His mandates* (Read Exodus 19:5; Deuteronomy 13:4; Acts 5:32.)
- *Accomplish His purposes* (Read Isaiah 14:27; Romans 8:28; Ephesians 1:7–10.)
- *Serve others in His name* (Read Genesis 27:29; Mark 10:45; 1 Peter 4:10.)
- *Be in His continual presence* (Read Psalms 16:11; 91:1; 1 Thessalonians 2:19.)

> *It is through our action and service*
> *that we show what love looks like.*

SPIRITUAL CHECKLIST

1. *Have you asked the Father in heaven to forgive you of personal sin? If the answer is no, then take the next few moments and confess the things you have done that have offended God.*

2. *Have you asked Jesus Christ into your life as Savior? If the answer is no, then repeat this simple prayer:*

> *"Father, I confess my sins before You and You alone.*
> *I ask that You come into my heart*
> *as Savior and Lord. Amen."*

3. *Are you set apart to God? If the answer is no, then list the obstacles you believe are keeping you from the presence of God.*

_____

_____

_____

_____

_____

_____

_____

STEP OF FAITH

Take a moment and personally commit to removing the confessed barriers that have kept you from living the victorious life of the believer. Have faith that God will give you the strength to change the things you have identified as roadblocks to your divine destiny. By doing so, you have begun your path to holiness. Remember, you cannot change what you will not confront.

> *You cannot change what you will not confront.*

Write down the step of faith you are willing to take.

_____

_____

_____

_____

_____

_____

PROCLAMATION

Father God, I invite Your Spirit into my life to show me the ways my thoughts and deeds have caused me to stand with the world rather than being set apart to You.

Give me the strength to turn away from any hindrance that keeps me from Your perfect will for my life. Cleanse me of any desires that surpass my longing for You so that I may be conformed to the image of Christ, my Savior. Amen.

Chapter 4

Sorrow—
My Sadness
for His Joy

Therefore you now have sorrow;
but I will see you again and your heart will rejoice,
and your joy no one will take from you.

JOHN 16:22

SCRIPTURAL FOUNDATIONS

Read 1 Samuel 1:6–9, 14–16.

Verses 6–7: *And [Hannah's] rival [Peninnah] also provoked her severely, to make her miserable, because the LORD had closed her womb. So it was, year by year, when [Peninnah] went up to the house of the LORD, that she provoked her; therefore [Hannah] wept and did not eat.*

From her first moments as a young bride, Hannah was eager to become a mother and give her husband a son who would perpetuate the family name. However, God chose to remain silent for nineteen long years in the face of the couple's prayers, for He had closed Hannah's womb. No doubt Hannah suffered countless sorrows and disappointments as those agonizing years of barrenness dragged on.[1]

The *Mishnah* (traditional Jewish law) stated that if a couple had been married for ten years without having any children, the husband was released to take another wife.[2] Hannah's distress was magnified when Elkanah took Peninnah as his second wife.

I can only imagine Hannah's tears of anguish as she lay alone in her bed each time her husband stayed the night in Peninnah's tent. How Hannah's heart must have ached when she heard the bittersweet sound of the birth cries of each of Elkanah and Peninnah's ten babies[3] . . . and when her nurturing husband lovingly held those children in his arms . . . and when she witnessed Elkanah laying hands on each of their heads to bestow the Sabbath blessing. Her husband was a Levite who faithfully taught his sons the ways of the Torah. Oh, how she longed to give her beloved Elkanah a son who could learn to serve the Lord all the days of his life!

Year after year Hannah went with Elkanah and the entire household to Shiloh to honor the festivals of the Lord, and year after year she returned from these times of celebration and worship further reminded of her emptiness whenever Peninnah looked her way with a taunting glance. The more Elkanah showed Hannah his favor and his love, the more Peninnah reviled Hannah and provoked her to tears.

Hannah's inadequacy consumed her as she carried the burden of social ridicule alone. Picture her as she walks inside the city gates and endures the accusing glares and whispered gossip; she is known as "Hannah, the Barren One." Still, Hannah trusted in the sovereign, all-powerful, all-knowing God. She remembered the stories of Sarah and Rebekah as she passed Rachel's tomb on her way to Shiloh. Just as God had given Sarah her son, Isaac; Rebekah her twin sons, Jacob and Esau; and Rachel her boys, Joseph and Benjamin, Hannah prayed and believed the Lord would also give her a son. The question was when.

Verse 8: *"Hannah, why do you weep? Why do you not eat? And why is your heart grieved? Am I not better to you than ten sons?"*

Elkanah knew the answer to the first three questions, for he had tried to comfort Hannah in her grief for many long years. He felt as frustrated about their plight as his cherished wife. He wanted to fix the situation, but he couldn't.

Hannah heard Elkanah's frustration when he asked her the last question. She probably sensed that he had resigned himself to never having a child with her, and he wanted Hannah to reconcile to the same. Perhaps that is when Hannah realized she stood alone with her faith in God.

Verse 9: *So Hannah arose after they had finished eating and drinking in Shiloh.*

On one of their annual pilgrimages to Shiloh to celebrate the Passover Feast, Elkanah and his household had made their peace offerings to God, and now Hannah's beloved husband wanted her to break her fast and eat with the rest of the family. I can imagine Hannah's struggle: she knows what she must do—submit to her husband's request even though her heart is not in it.

To deny our will and yield to the will of another requires inner strength that is only found when we first submit to God through the power of His grace. Hannah was overcome by sadness, yet rather than hardening herself in her sorrow, she submitted to Elkanah's request. She dried the tears from her eyes, composed herself, and joined the others at the table. Picture Hannah doing all she can to keep from crying as she sits with Elkanah, Peninnah, and all of their children and eats of the sacrifice without appetite or pleasure.

> *To deny our will and yield to the will of another requires inner strength that is only found when we first submit to God through the power of His grace.*

The Scriptures state that Hannah "arose" after she finished eating and drinking. Rabbinical scholars teach that Hannah didn't just physically get up but that she had ascended to another level in a spiritual sense, for she had met the conditions for answered prayer: she submitted to her husband, Hannah's direct spiritual authority (Ephesians 5:22); and she obediently ate of the sacrifice presented at the Holy Feast as mandated by the Lord (Deuteronomy 27:7). She then purposefully made her way to the tabernacle of meeting, the place where God had promised to receive His people (Exodus 29:43; 33:7). There she took a further step of faith, removing the oppressive yoke of barrenness off her shoulders and placing it on the altar of God.

Hannah may have been childless, but she was not prayerless. She was physically barren but not spiritually barren. She believed in God and His power, assured that in prayer she would find refuge from her pain.

It was time to keep her divine appointment—time to take her supplication to the Great I AM.

Verses 14–16: *Then Eli said to her, "How long will you make yourself drunk? Put away your wine from you." But Hannah replied, "No, my lord, I am a woman oppressed in spirit; I have drunk neither wine nor strong drink, but I have poured out my soul before the LORD. Do not consider your maidservant as a worthless woman, for I have spoken until now out of my great concern and provocation"* (NASB).

Once again, Hannah's anguish was misjudged. In a single day, she was reminded by Elkanah that worshipers were commanded to rejoice at the festivals of the Lord, and now she was wrongly accused of drunkenness by the High Priest! Hannah could have become even more disheartened and exasperated, but instead she respectfully and humbly explained herself to Eli.

Again, even through her sorrow, she chose to do what was right before the Lord, no matter what others did wrongfully to her. Hannah did not counter Eli's claim by justly accusing him of overlooking his own son's sins. Instead, she denied the charge, reverently addressed Eli, and revealed the nature of her prayer.

LIFE APPLICATION

Many are the afflictions of the righteous;
but the LORD delivers him out of them all.
PSALM 34:19

Sorrow is a natural feeling of deep distress, sadness, or grief caused by loss, disappointment, or other adversity. To Hannah, God seemed silent through those arduous years of suffering, yet how did she choose to respond to her sorrow?

To better answer that question, let's briefly review what the Scriptures say about sorrow and suffering. Sorrow is a God-given response to our suffering, which may be the result of:

1. Our wrong choices.
Read Genesis 16:1–5; 21:9–10. What consequences did Sarah suffer by implying that God had forgotten His promise of a child in her union with Abraham?

_____

_____

_____

_____

_____

2. Satan's attempt to bring out the worst in us.
Read James 1:12–16. What are the three stages of temptation?

_____

_____

_____

_____

_____

3. God's purpose to bring out the best in us.
Read Genesis 22:1–18; Psalm 66:10; Romans 5:3–5; James 1:3. List the positive results that God's testing produces in our lives.

_____

_____

_____

_____

_____

_____

_____

_____

_____

_____

4. A God-given response to personal loss.

God, the Grand Architect of our lives, created us with a natural means of dealing with our sorrows, and that inherent process is called mourning. Most of us who have walked through the valley of sorrow after the death of a loved one have felt the healing presence and comfort of our Blessed Hope leading us through our grief, just as He promised.

Read Nehemiah 8:10; Isaiah 49:13; Psalm 5:11; 31:24; 42:5; Titus 3:7; Romans 15:13; Hebrews 10:23; 1 Peter 1:21. Write down the promises God gives His children for a new tomorrow.

....

....

....

....

....

....

....

Our sorrow and suffering can also result in a closer, more intimate relationship with God. For one, our suffering helps us be more dependent on God.

Read Isaiah 50:10. What does Isaiah declare?

....

....

....

....

Read John 15:1–5. What message was Jesus Christ giving His disciples in these verses?

Now read the following scriptures regarding the fruit of our suffering. Reflect on how they may apply to your personal life.

- Repentance—2 Corinthians 7:9–10
- Patience—James 1:3–4
- Knowledge—Psalm 94:12–13
- Discipline—Hebrews 12:11
- Joy—Psalm 30:5
- Maturity—1 Peter 5:10

Our suffering can also be used to glorify God. Read John 9:1–3 and 11:1–4. In these passages, Jesus was rejecting the rabbinical teachings asserting that there was no suffering without sin and that God would punish children as a result of their parents' iniquity (sin).

How does Jesus's admonition help you deal with personal suffering and sorrow?

_____

_____

_____

_____

_____

_____

_____

_____

Good Grief vs. All-Consuming Grief

In this you greatly rejoice, though now for a little while, if need be, you have been grieved by various trials, that the genuineness of your faith, being much more precious than gold that perishes, though it is tested by fire, may be found to praise, honor, and glory at the revelation of Jesus Christ. (1 Peter 1:6–7)

It's natural for us to grieve over a tragic illness, the death of a marriage, the passing of a loved one, or shattered dreams (John 11:33–35). Good grief is like medicine to our soul—it's part of a necessary process that results in our healing. However, there comes a time when grieving must end and living must commence again. Our mourning should only last for a season; sorrow should never define a believer's personality or overwhelm their future.

> *Good grief is like medicine to our soul—*
> *it's part of a necessary process*
> *that results in our healing.*

If allowed, prolonged grief can grow like a prolific cancer robbing us of our joy and future hope. King David described the devastating results of all-consuming grief (Psalm 31:10). The prophet Jeremiah declared the Lord's deliverance from the destructive grips of grief (Jeremiah 31:13). And Isaiah reminded us of what Christ did to conquer our grief and sorrows (Isaiah 53:4).

When Ruth was mourning the death of her husband, Chilion, her wise and loving mother-in-law, Naomi, instructed Ruth to "wash yourself and anoint yourself, put on your best garment and go down to the threshing floor" (Ruth 3:3). This young widow had chosen the God of Naomi—the God of Abraham, Isaac, and Jacob—over the idols of Moab. Naomi instructed Ruth to cleanse herself from the past through the ritual bath (*mikvah*) and look to the future by putting on her best (Sabbath) clothing.

Immersion in the *mikvah* (water baptism) symbolized the turning away from one form of existence to accept one infinitely higher. It represented not only purification, revitalization, and rejuvenation but also—and perhaps primarily—rebirth.[4] The *mikvah* ritual is comparable to Christian water baptism, which symbolizes the death of the old nature and the rebirth of the new.

It was time for Hannah to cleanse her mind from past sorrows and transform her thoughts to a future hope.

Read Psalm 31:10 and list the detrimental effects of grief.

_____

_____

_____

_____

_____

_____

_____

_____

Remember this truth: God is able to redeem our sorrows and sufferings and exchange them with His joy and hope.

Good Grief Produces Hope

Why are you cast down, O my soul? And why are you disquieted within me? Hope in God, for I shall yet praise Him for the help of His countenance. (Psalm 42:5)

Biblical hope doesn't "wish for" anything—it *believes* in a positive outcome because of the One in whom that belief rests. It expects with confidence and cherishes a desire with anticipation even when circumstances don't seem optimistic, because our God is faithful. I *like* hope . . . it's the place I most enjoy living in.

> *Biblical hope doesn't "wish for" anything—*
> *it believes in a positive outcome*
> *because of the One in whom that belief rests.*

Surely Hannah struggled with doubt, her hope contending with her despair. *Will I be barren forever? How can I continue to endure the shame of my failure to bear a child? How long must I suffer from my grief?* Despite her deep sorrow, she held on to a divine assurance that God would hear her cry and answer her prayer.

Hannah had a choice to make. She could give up on her dream, or she could place her hope in the unshakable, unchanging grace of God, confident that He would answer her prayer in His omniscient way (Genesis 16:13). Hannah pressed forward in faith, and soon her sad countenance was transformed into liberating joy because of her trust in Him. No matter the outcome, Hannah knew that God would provide.

God is perfect love, and He is perfectly faithful; therefore, there is always reason for hope. God's everlasting faithfulness fuels our divine hope, lighting up our midnights.

Read Numbers 23:19; Psalm 71:5, 130:5; Proverbs 13:12; Jeremiah 17:7; Lamentations 3:24; Romans 5:5; Hebrews 11:1. Write what these verses mean to you.

Good Grief Produces Joy

You have loved righteousness and hated wickedness; therefore God, Your God, has anointed You with the oil of joy above Your fellows. (Psalm 45:7 NASB)

Joy is a secure state of contentment, confidence, and hope—and the fruit of believing in God's promises (Galatians 5:22). Joy is not a response to a temporary source of happiness; neither is it dependent on circumstances. In fact, supernatural joy is possible even when the entire world seems to be falling apart around us.

Our joy is found in God, for King David declared, "You make known to me the path of life; you will fill me with joy in your presence, with eternal pleasures at your right hand!" (Psalm 16:11 NIV). This should be the banner every woman of God carries in her heart regardless of the struggles she is facing.

> *Supernatural joy is possible*
> *even when the entire world*
> *seems to be falling apart around us.*

In time, Hannah realized that the source of her happiness would not come from a more understanding husband, a kinder Peninnah, or compassionate neighbors. Her wellspring of joy would come from God and God alone.

Hannah would soon sing a song of God's supernatural joy. For all of us, this is based on:

1. *God's Word.* The Word is God and God is the Word. There is no separation between them; they are ONE (Revelation 19:13).
   a. The Word is good seed (Matthew 13:23).
   b. The Word is always right (Psalm 33:4).
   c. The Word is incorruptible; it is everlasting, unchangeable, and immortal (1 Peter 1:23). And through His Word, God:
      - Redeems (Psalm 103:4)
      - Converts (Psalm 19:7)
      - Guides (John 16:13)
      - Heals (John 16:13)
      - Delivers (Psalm 34:17)
      - Provides everlasting life (John 5:24)

Write out the above scriptures and keep them somewhere where you will see them every day. In what ways do these verses improve your understanding of how essential God's Word is to the joyful, abundant life of the believer?

2. *His works.* All of God's works are just and righteous, which gives us reason to trust Him even more. As we obediently live a life of hope in the Lord, our dependence on and devotion to Him will grow. He is our Rock and Sustainer, and there is no wickedness in Him (Psalm 92:15).
    a. God's works are done in truth and justice (Daniel 4:37).
    b. They are perfect (Deuteronomy 32:4).
    c. They are just (Revelation 15:3).

Read the scriptures above and declare the good works of the Lord by writing down what each verse means to you.

_____

_____

_____

_____

_____

_____

_____

_____

3. *His lovingkindness.* God loves the world, and He displayed the extravagance of that love by sacrificing the life of His Son for our redemption.

Read Ephesians 1:3 and John 3:16. Define what God's lovingkindness means to you.

....

....

....

....

4. *His power.* Hannah knew that God has the power to give life, and she called upon Him to supply her desire for a child (Psalm 37:4). She had faith in God to fulfill what His Word said it would accomplish (Isaiah 55:11).

Read Jeremiah 32:17; Romans 13:1; 2 Corinthians 1:20. Meditate on these verses, absorbing them into your heart and mind, and then list the desires of your heart.

....

....

....

....

....

....

....

5. *His faithfulness.* God's mercies are infinite, and His faithfulness is eternal. These truths are the foundation of His nature and the source of our joy. Psalm 89:1 says, "I will sing of the mercies of the LORD forever; with my mouth will I make known Your faithfulness to all generations."

It is when we turn our hearts to the truth of God's character that His promises become reality. In order for Hannah's shroud of mourning to be transformed, she needed to put on her garment of praise by giving thanks to the Lord for His enduring faithfulness (Isaiah 61:3).

The Psalms are rich in declaring God's faithfulness. Read through a few right now and list the ones that are meaningful to you. Allow them to become a wellspring of living water yielding unending joy.

_____

_____

_____

_____

_____

_____

Though Hannah had lived in distress for years, she ultimately understood that being consumed by her situation would not bring resolution. Surely she cried out to God to stop Peninnah's spiteful taunting, yet Peninnah continued nonetheless. Surely Hannah had wept many a night, begging God for more empathy from her husband and consideration from her community, yet it seemed as if both understood her sorrow less and less.

Any time we perpetually dwell on our afflictions rather than God's faithfulness, we are destined to despair. Fixing our eyes on the problem is a subtle tool used by the Adversary to dig the pit of depression even deeper. However, praise is the heavenly spade we can use to throw off the lies and accusations that the Enemy heaps on us.

LIFE STORIES

A grief-stricken widow sat in the sterile family waiting room of a New York hospital in stunned silence. Her only child had died moments earlier, and now tears of anguish rolled down her face as she attempted to listen to the consoling words of the charge nurse.

The mother was frozen by grief and disbelief; she could not imagine life without her little girl. Her world had revolved around her daughter, especially after the untimely death of her husband in the war. Struggling to take every breath, she could hardly stand the agonizing pain of her broken heart.

A few minutes passed, and the nurse came back into the room holding the hand of a shabbily dressed little boy with tousled black hair. She sat him at the far end of the room and walked back to the distraught mother as the child quietly sobbed. The nurse placed her hand on the mother's shoulder and asked if she had noticed the pint-sized boy slumped in his chair across the long room. The mother had not perceived anything other than the darkening realization that her daughter was gone.

The nurse began to tell the child's story. The boy and his mother had lost all their relatives in the concentration camps of

Europe and had come to America with only the clothes on their back. Even though they lived in a dingy one-room apartment, they were grateful to have each other. A week earlier, the mother had been brought to the hospital by ambulance, unconscious after suffering from a high fever for several days.

The nurse continued, "This poor child has not left his mother's side since she was admitted to the hospital. Day after day we have watched him stare into her face, waiting for her to wake up and call his name. Ten minutes ago his mother died, leaving him with no home and no family. I now have to tell him that the authorities will be by in a few hours to take him to the nearby orphanage."

The distraught mother looked into the nurse's eyes and slowly turned her attention toward the small figure pitifully slouched in the chair across the room. The wise nurse continued, "I wonder if you could help me break the news to this small child of seven?"

As if the room were suddenly lit by a warm light of hope, the grieving mother dried her tears with her dress, stood, and walked over to the sobbing little boy and wrapped her loving arms around him. Then she quietly led the homeless boy to her childless home, and the sorrow they both knew was transformed by the hope they found in each other.[5]

And *that's* what love looks like . . .

Very few of us have experienced this kind of sorrow; some of us, however, have dealt with even more. In every situation, God is our Deliverer from the debilitating presence of darkness. We must choose to stop looking at our lives through the dim glass of sadness and begin to see clearly with the Light from above, for there is no shadow of turning in Christ Jesus (James 1:17). In His presence is the fullness of joy.

> You will show me the path of life;
> In Your presence is fullness of joy;
> At Your right hand are pleasures forevermore.
> (Psalm 16:11)

SPIRITUAL CHECKLIST

1. *Far too many of us listen to the condemning voice of the Accuser above the voice of our Redeemer. Write down the accusations with which Satan is tormenting you, and then declare each indictment "null and void" through the power of Christ. Read Psalm 109:28–31 and Revelation 12:10.*

2. Many of us are guilty of speaking curses over ourselves and our loved ones. But Scripture teaches, "Let the words of my mouth and the meditation of my heart be acceptable in Your sight, O LORD, my strength and my Redeemer" (Psalm 19:14). Confess everything that you have spoken over yourself and those you love that contradicts the Word of God.

_____

_____

_____

_____

_____

_____

_____

3. It is beneficial to honestly acknowledge your grief and sadness before the Lord, but don't dwell there. Leave that place of want and despair and enter into His courts with thanksgiving and praise, where you can hear "the voice of joy and the voice of gladness, the voice of the bridegroom and the voice of the bride, the voice of those who will say: 'Praise the LORD of hosts, for the LORD is good, for His mercy endures forever'—and of those who will

bring the sacrifice of praise into the house of the LORD*" (Jeremiah
33:11). Write down a personal declaration of praise to the Lord
by simply thanking Him for all He has done in your life.*

_____

_____

_____

_____

_____

_____

_____

_____

_____

_____

_____

_____

> *O Lord, open my lips, and my mouth
> shall show forth Your praise.*
>
> PSALM 51:15

STEP OF FAITH

Christ took our sorrow and substituted it with His joy when He died on the cross of Calvary. This Great Exchange allowed us to be free from the attacks of despair and enduring depression that enslave so many.

What step of faith do you need to take to begin to rise out of the valley of sorrow and up to the mount of supernatural joy?

_____

_____

_____

_____

_____

_____

_____

_____

> *But let all those rejoice who put their trust in You.*
> *Let them ever shout for joy, because*
> *You defend them; let those also*
> *who love Your name be joyful in You.*
>
> PSALM 5:11

PROCLAMATION

Father, forgive me for heeding the voice of the Enemy above Your truth. I will no longer listen to the lies of Satan nor be held captive by his destructive accusations. Instead, I will attend to the promises found in Your Word.

Forgive me for speaking negative words over myself and my loved ones. I affirm that I will speak only words of blessing, encouragement, and hope—or say nothing at all.

I will praise You for Your merciful goodness even while I walk through the valley of sorrow. I have been set free from the grief and regrets of the past, and I look forward to the good things that You have declared over my life and the lives of my loved ones.

I will exchange my sorrow for Your joy and have faith that You will hear my prayer and grant my heartfelt petitions according to Your Word. I receive my breakthrough now in the mighty name of Jesus! Amen.

Chapter 5

Supplication— The Silent Cry

> *Be anxious for nothing, but in everything*
> *by prayer and supplication, with thanksgiving,*
> *let your requests be made known to God.*
> PHILIPPIANS 4:6

SCRIPTURAL FOUNDATIONS

Read 1 Samuel 1:9–13, 17–18.

Verse 9: *Now Eli the priest was sitting on the seat by the doorpost of the tabernacle of the LORD.*

Eli was from the tribe of Levi and held the office of Judge and High Priest in Shiloh (1 Samuel 1:9). The first mention of him in Scripture occurs with the story of Hannah and her treasured Samuel.

The High Priest was required to provide the oracles to the

people as conveyed by God by means of the Urim and Thummim in the breastplate on the linen ephod (Leviticus 8:7–8), to make sacrificial offerings on the Day of Atonement (Leviticus 16:3), to oversee the duties of the sanctuary (Numbers 3:38), to supervise the census (Numbers 26:1–2), to teach God's laws (Deuteronomy 33:10), to anoint kings (2 Kings 11:12), and to intercede for the people (Ezra 9:5).

Verse 10: *And she was in bitterness of soul, and prayed to the* Lord *and wept in anguish.*

This verse speaks of deep hurt, of tears, and of anguish. Hannah was exasperated, exhausted, and felt abandoned. Her "bitterness of soul" led her to cry out to God. She wept from her heart just as Sarah (Genesis 11:30), Rebekah (Genesis 25:21), and Rachel (Genesis 30:22) had when they too prayed for God to deliver them from their barrenness.

This woman of God was weary of waiting. Her desire for a child had gone unanswered for over nineteen years, she was drained from listening to Peninnah's taunts, and now Elkanah was asking her to resign herself to the fact that she would be childless for the rest of her life. It was time for her to take decisive action.

Verse 11: *Then she made a vow and said, "O* Lord *of hosts, if You will indeed look on the affliction of Your maidservant and remember me, and not forget Your maidservant, but will give Your maidservant a male child, then I will give him to the* Lord *all the days of his life, and no razor shall come upon his head."*

Hannah had carefully prepared for her crucial encounter with God, and within a few moments after walking to the doorpost of the tabernacle of meeting, she presented her vow to the Almighty.

She wrapped herself in humility and addressed *Hashem* as the "Lord of hosts." Rabbinical scholars state that Hannah was the first person since God created His world to use this phrase.[1] With these words, Hannah undeniably proclaimed that the God she served was the Master of the universe, the Ruler of all.

The Lord of hosts was well known to the children of Israel. He was the Great Covenant Maker to Abraham (Genesis 15:18). He was the Deliverer to the Israelites of Egypt (Exodus 13:18). He was the Law Giver to Moses (Deuteronomy 4:13). He was Ruth's Kinsman-Redeemer (Ruth 4). And He was Hannah's only hope for a son. Hannah called on the Lord to look upon her—to remember and not forget her. Then she presented her twofold vow.

A vow is a solemn promise made to God to perform, or to abstain from performing, a certain act. The first portion of her promise was that her son would be devoted to God's service in the sanctuary, not for a set number of years as was the law of the Levites (Numbers 4:3), but for life. Second, he would serve as a Nazarite—one who would abstain from any form of self-indulgence and instead lead a holy and consecrated life (Numbers 6:1–21). Through this noble gesture Hannah gave up the right of future claim and guidance over her child. It was not possible for her to give any more; her heartfelt vow was the maximum form of self-surrender.

Hannah poured out her soul and called on the Lord to intervene in the laws of nature and let her bring forth a son. She easily could have asked the Lord to cause her husband to sympathize with her more, or to change Peninnah's heart toward her, or even to take away her own sorrow, but she chose to stand pure before *Hashem* and present her supplication and vow.

Hannah prayed not where men could hear; instead, she offered her supplication to the Lord in quiet intimacy—a petition known to God alone.

Hannah would later influence her son's prayer life, for Samuel would prophesy with the words: "Thus said *the LORD of hosts*" (1 Samuel 15:2, emphasis mine). And observant Jews use her prayer as a model to this day: they stand while they pray in a reverent frame of mind; and they pray softly enough so others cannot hear, but not silently, for the words of the prayer must be clearly enunciated.[2] Think of it. God caused the earnest prayers of a virtuous woman to inspire the way the righteous pray for centuries to come.

> *Think of it. God caused the earnest prayers of a virtuous woman to inspire the way the righteous pray for centuries to come.*

We all come to a time when we have no choice but to cry out to God from the depths of our heart. I was diagnosed with breast cancer on the day before Thanksgiving in 2008. After the shock of hearing that dreadful word I was immediately tormented by fear, doubt, and guilt.

I was the pastor's wife; shouldn't I effortlessly sail through this battle?

It was not the case. The Enemy tortured me with my grandmother's and sister's deaths from cancer years before. He relentlessly taunted me with my younger sister's own battle with this evil disease two years prior. I remember as if it were yesterday . . . I closed the doors to my home, shut out the world, and cried out to the Lord with the following prayer that I recorded in my journal:

> Father God, fear, doubt, worry and anxiety battle against me. Your Word declares that I should cast my fears upon You. I cry out to You to replace my fear with trust, my doubt with faith, and my worry with hope. Amen.

After my prayer I began to praise God for His healing. I turned the corner that day and stood once again on my spiritual legs. After being surrounded with love and support from my family and friends I underwent a double mastectomy, and on January 19, 2009 I was declared cancer-free. I still have that tattered prayer journal and I read it often to remind me of my divine journey with the Lord.

I cried out to God. He heard my prayer, and He answered. Hallelujah!

Verses 12–13: *Now it came about, as she continued praying before the LORD, that Eli was watching her mouth. As for Hannah, she was speaking in her heart, only her lips were moving, but her voice was not heard. So Eli thought she was drunk* (NASB).

The moral conditions of Shiloh at this time were abysmal. Sadly, Eli's two sons, Hophni and Phinehas, took full advantage of their privileged position and dishonored the priesthood through all forms of bribery, corruption, and immorality. The father rebuked his sons, but not strongly enough, for they never turned from their wicked ways. (Read 1 Samuel 2:12–17, 22–25.) Still, it was the responsibility of the High Priest to safeguard the tabernacle; he was the guardian of the sanctuary and the chief authority regarding Judaic law and religious principles. This is why Eli was sitting at the doorpost of the tabernacle when Hannah offered her prayer.

Seeing Hannah's lips move yet hearing no words, he instantly assumed she was intoxicated and wrongly accused her of being drunk. Eli had become so insensitive to genuine supplication that he was guilty of judging externals rather than recognizing that this woman might be offering a chaste, heartfelt prayer.

Verse 17: *Then Eli answered and said, "Go in peace, and the God of Israel grant your petition which you have asked of Him."*

After hearing Hannah's sincere response to his false accusation, Eli then blessed and assured her that her earnest prayer had been heard by God.

Verse 18: *She said, "Let your maidservant find favor in your sight." So the woman went her way and ate, and her face was no longer sad.*

The word *favor* here refers to a special standing or privilege with God or man. Hannah received confirmation that her prayer had been heard through the High Priest's blessing.

Why was she "no longer sad"? What happened?

Have you ever prayed to God and felt a deep peace? You just "know in your knower" that He has heard your prayer and that His answer is on the way? That is exactly what Hannah felt. Through her supplication, Hannah left her burden at the throne of God and put her complete trust in Him. She walked away from the tabernacle of meeting with the blessed assurance that the Great I AM had heard her cry, and this supernatural confidence was reflected in her joyful countenance.

> *Prayer is not a formula but a divine prescription that will bring healing, restoration, provision, guidance, and comfort.*

LIFE APPLICATION

*For the eyes of the LORD are on the righteous,
and His ears are open to their prayers.*

1 PETER 3:12

Prayer in Judaism is called a *mitzvah*. A *mitzvah* is the fulfillment of the commandments of Jewish law. It can also refer to a good and worthy deed. If a person has to travel miles to keep the Sabbath, it is not considered a good deed; it is expected of an observant Jew to do what it takes to obey the Sabbath law. However, prayer is not the result of duty but instead reflects a desire for a more personal, intimate relationship with the Creator. This sacrificial effort is considered a *mitzvah*.

The Lord is omnipresent—meaning He is in every aspect of our lives, whether in times of trouble or triumph (read Psalm 139:7–10). Yet we must invite His presence in all situations through prayer. Prayer is a belief that God can be petitioned to intervene in the laws of nature, such as in the birth of Isaac to a ninety-one-year-old Sarah (read Genesis 17:17–21); the parting of the Red Sea (read Exodus 14); in world events such as the redemption of

Queen Esther and the Jewish people of ancient Persia (read Esther 8–9); the miraculous rebirth of the nation of Israel (read Isaiah 66:8); as well as in a multitude of ways in the everyday lives of His people.

List specific ways God has intervened in your life.

_____

_____

_____

_____

_____

_____

_____

_____

_____

Prayer is not a formula but a divine prescription that will bring healing, restoration, provision, guidance, and comfort. Establishing a more intimate relationship with God does not come through memorized or repetitious recitations but through personal conversations from the heart. Most importantly, we must pray to God in faith, believing that He hears and He will answer.

Prayer involves commitment to our cause and to Christ. We can pray alone, pray with others, or have others pray for us. Whatever the case, we must recognize God's voice, obey what He mandates, and invoke His presence and power in our lives (Exodus 15:26).

Prayer is vital to the life of the believer. Prayer is sacred—it is how we draw near to God.

Types of Prayer

Therefore I exhort first of all that supplications, prayers, intercessions, and giving of thanks be made for all men. (1 Timothy 2:1)

1. *The Prayer of Agreement* (also known as corporate prayer):

   These all [the disciples] continued with one accord in prayer and supplication, with the women and Mary the mother of Jesus, and with His brothers. (Acts 1:14)

   The Lord promises to command His blessings when His people gather in unity (Psalm 133). In response to this promise, the women of Cornerstone Church host an annual Solemn Assembly. During this sacred time we corporately pray over our church, city, state, and nation, and for the peace of Jerusalem (2 Chronicles 7:14; Psalm 122:6). We set ourselves apart for seven hours of fervent, consecrated prayer unto the Lord, uniting with full expectation that what is prayed according to His will is heard by God and will be answered.

List the specific needs of your church, city, state, and nation. Come in agreement with your Bible study group and set a time to pray over these needs. End your session by praying for the peace of Jerusalem.

....

....

....

....

....

....

....

....

....

....

....

2.   *The Prayer of Thanksgiving:*

Let them sacrifice the sacrifices of thanksgiving,
And declare His works with rejoicing. (Psalm 107:22)

Thanksgiving is the banner every believer is created to live under. We should always come into the presence of God in a spirit of gratitude even at the most challenging times of our lives. One simple way to develop the spirit of gratefulness is to think on the good things that have come to our lives through the hand of God.

List the ways the Lord has blessed your life and the lives of your loved ones.

_____

_____

_____

_____

_____

_____

_____

_____

_____

_____

3. *The Prayer of Worship*:

> Give unto the LORD the glory due to His name;
> Worship the LORD in the beauty of holiness. (Psalm 29:2)

The prayer of worship is similar to the prayer of thanksgiving. The difference is that thanksgiving focuses on what God has *done* while worship focuses on who God *is*.

Some believers erroneously worship God's attributes instead of God and God alone. For example, if "holiness" is the subject matter of a Bible teaching, the participants must not worship the attribute of "holiness" but worship *God*, who is holy.

With that in mind, take a moment to consider some of the glorious attributes of our God—those traits that define His nature. God is:

- *Sovereign.* He is the ultimate source of all supreme power and authority. The Lord is above all things, before all things, and He can accomplish all things. God answers to no one. He and He alone is sovereign, and He and He alone is worthy of our worship. Deuteronomy 4:39 declares that there is no one like God, "Therefore know this day, and consider it in your heart, that the LORD Himself is God in heaven above and on the earth beneath; there is no other."

Read each of the following psalms in their entirety: 18, 33, 97, and 104. Write down what these passages say about God's sovereignty.

- *Wise.* "Wisdom is the ability to create perfect ends and to achieve these ends by the most perfect means."[3] King David proclaimed, "To Him [God] who by wisdom made the heavens, for His mercy endures forever . . ." (Psalm 136:5). King Solomon declared, "For the LORD gives wisdom; from His mouth come knowledge and understanding" (Proverbs 2:6). And Paul described God's wisdom in 1 Corinthians 2:7: "But we speak the wisdom of God in a mystery, the hidden wisdom which God ordained before the ages for our glory." My husband often says that God is too loving to be unkind and too wise to make a mistake.

List other scriptures that declare God's wisdom.

....

....

....

....

- *Love.* Love doesn't define God; God defines love. God's selfless love was manifested by the sacrifice of His only Son for the redemption of our sins (John 3:16). The two most important truths to remember about this attribute are that, first, we must accept that God loves us and wants only the best for us. "But God, who is rich in mercy, because of His great love with which He loved us, even when we were dead in trespasses, made us alive together with Christ" (Ephesians 2:4–5). The second is that we are commanded to be a reflection of God's love to others. 1 John 4:8 declares that "he who does not

love does not know God, for God is love." God's love is immeasurable, indestructible, unconditional, unwavering, and
undeserved. God rules in love; love is His very nature.

List other scriptures that declare God's love.

_____

_____

_____

_____

- *Faithful.* Faithfulness is defined as a steadfast allegiance, a loyal
  adherence to a promise; it is a binding assurance. God is faithful to His Word; He will see to it that what He has promised
  will come to pass. God does not lie; what He has said in His
  Word about Himself is true. Moses spoke of God's faithfulness
  in Deuteronomy 7:9: "Therefore know that the LORD your
  God, He is God, the faithful God who keeps covenant and
  mercy for a thousand generations with those who love Him
  and keep His commandments."

List other scriptures that declare God's faithfulness.

_____

_____

_____

_____

- *Omniscient.* God knows all things past, present, and future. There is no limit to His knowledge, for He knows everything before it happens, from beginning to end. God knows all there is to know; it is impossible to hide anything from Him. It is beyond our comprehension to define all God knows! Romans 11:33 proclaims, "Oh, the depth of the riches both of the wisdom and knowledge of God! How unsearchable are His judgments and His ways past finding out!"

List other scriptures that describe God's omniscience.

_____

_____

- *Holy.* Holiness is what sets God apart from all other gods. God *is* holy. He is pure; He is righteous; He is truth and perfect justice. There is absolutely no sin in God. Moses acknowledged God's holiness in Exodus 15:11 when he asked, "Who is like You, O Lord, among the gods? Who is like You, glorious in holiness, fearful in praises, doing wonders?"

List other scriptures that declare God's holiness.

_____

_____

_____

- *Eternal.* God is the Alpha and the Omega, the Beginning and the End. The Great I AM is self-existing; He was before time began, and He will always be. God's attributes are eternal as well. They never change; they are everlasting to everlasting. All of His creation is bound by time, but God transcends time. Eternity is God's signature. It is who He is. It is written in Deuteronomy 33:27: "The eternal God is your refuge, and underneath are the everlasting arms."

List the scriptures that declare the eternal nature of God.

....

....

....

....

4. *The Prayer of Consecration*:

And when He had sent the multitudes away, He went up on the mountain by Himself to pray. Now when evening came, He was alone there. (Matthew 14:23)

Then great multitudes came to Him, having with them the lame, blind, mute, maimed, and many others; and they laid them down at Jesus' feet, and He healed them. So the multitude marveled when they saw the mute speaking, the maimed made whole, the lame walking, and the blind seeing; and they glorified the God of Israel. (Matthew 15:30–31)

Jesus prepared Himself for His divine mission through consecrated prayer. *Consecration* means "to make or declare sacred, to be set apart to serve in dedication to the One who is Holy." This type of prayer gives believers the opportunity to be set apart for His divine assignment, bringing glory to God and God alone.

Moses met with God and was set apart to receive the Ten Commandments (Exodus 24:2); Ruth set herself apart by praying herself into the family of God (Ruth 1:16); Esther and Daniel respectively fasted and prayed and were set apart to save a nation and to warn the generations to come (Esther 4:16; Daniel 10:2–3, 7–8); Mary prayed and was set apart to bring forth the Savior of mankind (Luke 1:29–38); and the apostle Paul prayed and was set apart to preach the gospel to all the world (2 Corinthians 9:3–6, 20).

Make a list of fellow Christians who have prayed to the Lord and been set apart by Him to do mighty works for the kingdom of God (examples: Corrie ten Boom, Dietrich Bonhoeffer, Mother Teresa, Billy Graham).

5.   *The Prayer of Intercession*:

Therefore I exhort first of all that supplications, prayers, intercessions, and giving of thanks be made for all men. (1 Timothy 2:1)

Intercession is the act of praying to God on behalf of others. Jesus serves as our perfect example; He prayed to His Father for the sake of mankind time and time again, and He quickens us to do the same (read Romans 8:34; Ephesians 6:18).

A good example of intercessory prayer is the dedicated group of men and women in our church who are part of the WE FAST prayer team. These are trusted individuals who have committed to pray and fast one day a week for the confidential needs of the body of Christ. When a dire situation is brought to their attention (such as a terminal disease or the need for supernatural protection or personal intervention) from anywhere around the world, this team goes into action and collectively prays over each concern until the answer comes. Anyone with a heart willing to enter the throne room of God for the sake of others and who believes that the Lord can accomplish the impossible is welcome to join.

List those whose needs the Lord brings to your mind and commit yourself to intercede on their behalf.

6.   *The Prayer of Supplication*:

> And the LORD said to him: "I have heard your prayer and
> your supplication that you have made before Me; I have
> consecrated this house which you have built to put My
> name there forever, and My eyes and My heart will be
> there perpetually." (1 Kings 9:3)

God heard King Solomon's prayer, and He will hear yours.
Supplication is derived from the Latin verb *supplicare*, which
means "to plead humbly." It is applicable to any situation
in which we entreat God to bestow His favor on us. And
Hannah's prayer is one of the finest of Scripture's examples.

*Read 1 Kings 8:28–59; 9:3. Write down what King Solomon said
about supplications to God.*

_____

_____

_____

_____

_____

_____

_____

7.   *The Prayer of Faith*:

And the prayer of faith will save the sick, and the Lord will raise him up. And if he has committed sins, he will be forgiven. (James 5:15)

Christ charged us to pray in faith. He emphasized this responsibility when He said, "Therefore I say to you, whatever things you ask when you pray, believe that you receive them, and you will have them" (Mark 11:24). *Everything* that comes with the redemption of Jesus Christ is available to *all believers* who present their supplication *in faith* and who are ready to receive it!

Paul described Abraham's faith in Romans 4:20–21 when he said, "[Abraham] did not waver at the promise of God through unbelief, but was strengthened in faith, giving glory to God, and being fully convinced that what He had promised He was able to perform." Like Abraham, we are to call those things that are not as though they were, until they are!

The prayer of faith has no "ifs" in it!

It does not matter how we pray, when we pray, how loudly we pray, or how often we pray . . . If we don't believe God will answer our prayer, it won't be answered!

List those things that you struggle to believe God for.

_____

_____

_____

_____

_____

_____

_____

Remember this truth: the prayer of faith has no "ifs" in it! There is no question in the will of God concerning salvation of the lost, healing of the sick, provision for the needy, restoration of broken relationships, or deliverance of the oppressed. Our prayers to the God of Abraham, Isaac, and Jacob—when prayed in Jesus's name and through the power of His blood—are effective! Pastor Hagee says, "Every prayer prayed in the Lord's name is like a supernatural atomic bomb!"

> *Every prayer prayed in the Lord's name*
> *is like a supernatural atomic bomb!*

Many of us are ignorant of the power we have in Christ, made possible by His death and resurrection. It is important to accept that we, as believers, inherit supernatural authority the moment we accept Jesus as Savior and Lord. Therefore, it is our responsibility to acknowledge this divine right and activate its power in prayer (read Matthew 17:20).

The Authority of the Believer

But God, being rich in mercy, because of His great love with which He loved us, even when we were dead in our transgressions, made us alive together with Christ (by grace you have been saved), and raised us up with Him, and seated us with Him in the heavenly places in Christ Jesus, so that in the ages to come He might show the surpassing riches of His grace in kindness toward us in Christ Jesus. (Ephesians 2:4–7 NASB)

God's authority is available to every one of His children.[4] However, too many believers have underestimated, and most definitely underutilized, this power. Once this authority is activated through prayer, believers can face the Enemy in spiritual battle without fear or uncertainty.

Christ established three essential truths through His death at the cross:

1. He was completely submitted to the Father.
2. He was the perfect atonement for our sin.
3. He crushed the enemies of Divine Authority.

After Christ defeated death, hell, and the grave, He took His position of authority at the right hand of God, and we are entitled to occupy that same eminent place "with Him" (Ephesians 2:4–7).

Qualifications of Authority

The authority of the believer is not earned but is imparted by our Father at the moment of our salvation. It is not a gift for a few—instead, it is God's delegated power available for all who have accepted Christ as Savior.

Our authority is activated through:

1. *Faith.* In order to live in the authority of Christ, we must believe that His Word is true. When we have an intimate relationship with God and His Word, then we accept that nothing is impossible for those of us who believe.

2. *Humility.* A humble spirit brought us to the cross of Christ, and that same spirit keeps us in His presence. The more victories we have, the more we must clothe ourselves in Christ's humility so we can give God *all* the glory for *all* answered prayer.

3. *Boldness.* True boldness is faith in full manifestation; it requires us to have the courage to walk by faith and not by sight.

4. *Fear of God.* This type of fear is not a form of terror or distress but is defined as the awesome reverence of God. Imagine a God so loving that He imparts His *throne power* to His children. However, God will never share His glory; therefore, we must acknowledge that if He is the source of the power, then He is also the source of the victory and should be the focus of our praise!

5. *The Armor of God.* Our place of power and protection are only found at His delegated seat of authority. To maintain this position, we must daily put on the full armor of God. The Enemy cannot enter into this sacred place, nor can he remove us from this safeguarded position. However,

if we choose to vacate this exalted seat, we remove ourselves from God's imparted authority and supernatural protection; once His covering is gone, we are open to the Enemy's attack.

Read Ephesians 6:11–18 to better understand the components of the armor briefly described below:

- *Girdle of Truth* (v. 14). The girdle of truth provides clear understanding of God's Word. It is like a belt; it keeps the rest of the armor in place.

- *Breastplate of Righteousness* (v. 14). The breastplate of righteousness protects our heart and is reflected in our obedience to the Word of God.

- *Feet Shod with the Gospel of Peace* (v. 15). The faithful proclamation of the gospel is shown through our deeds.

- *Shield of Faith* (v. 16). The shield of faith allows believers to stay under the protection of the blood of Christ.

- *Helmet of Salvation* (v. 17). Also known as the Hope of our Salvation (1 Thessalonians 5:8), this is displayed by our confidence in the coming of the Lord, which is our ultimate redemption.

- *Sword of the Spirit* (v. 17). The sword of the Spirit is the use of the Word of God in spiritual battle.

- *Prayer without Ceasing* (v. 18). Our presence should be constantly before the throne of God in supplication, intercession, and thanksgiving.

> *Prayer is vital to the life of the believer.*
> *Prayer is sacred—it is how we draw near to God.*

Prayer is a believer's lifeline. It is our ability to speak to our Father in heaven from the innermost part of our being. Our most effective prayers come from the heart, not from our minds or a book. If our prayers are not borne of the pure heart, the humble heart, and the believing heart, they are fruitless.

Every true heart-prayer that our heavenly Father accepts first came from Him.

LIFE STORIES

Jesus taught in parables—stories that clearly communicated His message. Because prayer takes various forms and has various targets, I believe the following short story is in order to help illustrate heartfelt prayer.

The White Birds

A woman dreamt that she walked into an old prayer chapel where she knelt, offered her prayer, and sat back in silence to appreciate the beauty of the ancient building. As she glanced around the cavernous room, she noticed other silent, kneeling figures scattered among the pews.

She sat in awe at the brilliance of the sun's golden hue that streamed through the stained glass windows surrounding the church's vaulted dome. Her admiring gaze finally rested on a wide-open door that let in a gentle summer breeze accented by the fragrance of the church's flower gardens. It was indeed a beautiful setting.

Suddenly, close to the bench where she was sitting, a gentle whir of wings came from a little white bird fluttering about in the dimly lit nave. As the woman observed the creature fly around with uncertainty, she at times was sure that it would fall to the ground.

But gradually the bird gathered strength, rose toward the ceiling, and finally, with a purposeful sweep of its wings, sped upward and out through one of the open windows into the sunshine.

Then the woman shifted her glance back to the others who were singularly scattered throughout the chapel. She noticed something she had not seen before: by the side of each worshiper, close to the stone floor, a little white bird hovered.

She saw one of these winged beauties rise and attempt to reach the ceiling, also flying around in circles, futilely beating its wings against the richly decorated windows above. However, this little bird sank to the stone floor, exhausted and still.

A few seconds later, yet another bird rose from the ground. This one flew swiftly and easily, and for a moment it seemed that it would reach the open window and soar into the sky beyond. Unexpectedly, the bird whirled around and fell to the ground with a *thud*, as if it had been shot. The woman rose from her pew and walked in the direction of the fallen bird and found it lying dead.

She went back to her seat, and this time she noticed an ugly bird, its white feathers dirty and unkempt, rise from the floor. At first this bird labored heavily, but it soon gathered speed, for it was strong, and then it soared up and out into the sunlit world beyond the walls of the great church.

She looked again at the other individuals praying near her and noticed one woman kneeling very reverently. By that woman's side, stoically perched, was a very beautiful white bird. Looking more closely, the observer noticed that the bird's eyes were blank, its wings stiff; it was a lifeless shell.

At that very moment, a gentle hum of wings a few feet away caught her attention. Another bird was now lifting off steadily from the ground. At first it flew with some effort, but then it gathered its strength and soared straight up past the carved angels, which seemed to be crying "Hallelujah!" to one another across the dim spaces of the church. The beautiful little white bird then flew through the open window into the blue sky, where it was soon lost to sight.

Pondering all that she had witnessed, the woman looked around again, only this time she saw an angel standing close by. He was tall and strong, with a face showing great kindness, wisdom, and compassion. The woman walked toward him and whispered, "Can you enlighten me on these little white birds?"

The angel responded, "God has appointed me as the guardian of this place of prayer. The white birds are the outward signs of the prayers of those who come to offer their supplications. The first bird, which found it difficult to rise but then succeeded, is the prayer of a woman who has come here straight from a very busy life. She has little time to herself; in fact, she usually comes here in the middle of her workday. She has a great many family responsibilities, and her mind was full of distractions when she first knelt down and tried to pray. But she persevered, for her heart is right with God. He knew her prayer was from the soul, offered in faith, so her prayer reached Him."

"And what about the bird that flew around in circles?" asked the woman.

The angel responded soberly, "That was the prayer of a woman who thinks of no one but herself. Even in prayer, she only asks for material things, personal success, and worldly desires. She tries to use God for her own ends . . . People think she is very religious—but sadly, her prayer does not reach God at all."

"And why did the third bird fall to the ground as if it had been shot?" asked the woman.

The angel looked sad as he replied, "That woman began her prayer with good intentions, but suddenly she remembered a grudge against someone who had offended her. She forgot her prayer and brooded in bitter resentment until her anger killed her petition."

The angel continued, "And the ugly bird is the prayer of a woman who doesn't have much tact. Some may even call her prayers unduly bold and almost presumptuous, but God sees that her faith is real; her prayer is heartfelt and her belief in God pure, so her prayer reaches Him."

"And the beautiful lifeless bird that never stirred from the ground at all?" asked the woman.

"That," said the angel, "is a beautifully composed prayer. The language is flawless; the thought is doctrinally sound; the woman offered it with the greatest solemnity and outward reverence. But she never meant a word of it—it was only intended for others to notice. Even as she perfectly recited the words, her thoughts were on her own affairs, so her prayer could not reach God."

"What about the last bird that flew up and out the window so easily?"

The angel smiled. "I think you know," he said gently. "That is the prayer of a woman whose whole heart and will are set upon God. Her prayer was unhindered and went straight to the throne of heaven."[5]

᠎᠎᠎

Derek Prince preached about prayer at Cornerstone Church many times. His summarized points about prayer ring true in our study of Hannah: any time you pray, stand on this ageless truth: every prayer of a Christian, prayed in faith, according to God's Word, based on His promises, prayed in the name of Jesus, inspired by the Holy Spirit—whether for temporal or spiritual blessing—is or will be fully answered.

And *that's* what love looks like.

SPIRITUAL CHECKLIST

One of the questions I first asked after accepting Christ as Savior is the same question new believers now ask me: "How do I pray?" Most of us like formulas or absolutes, but God desires prayers from the heart. As I stated before, prayers are placed in a pure heart by a righteous God (read 2 Samuel 7).

The disciples asked Jesus the same question, and He answered them by teaching the model prayer that is known as the Lord's Prayer (read Luke 11:1–4). My mother-in-law, Vada Hagee, would often say, "I pray the Lord's Prayer every day. If it was good enough for Jesus, then it's good enough for me."

We took her example to heart here at Cornerstone Church and have set aside a noon prayer time every day to say the Lord's Prayer. Anyone in our church or extended ministry around the world may join us. It provides an opportunity for both daily and corporate prayer.

A checklist that helps us on the right path to prayer is the ACTS method, which once again is merely a tool to aid us in coming into the presence of God.

- Adoration and Praise—Open your time of prayer with praise unto the Lord for who He is! "How awesome are Your works!" (Psalm 66:3).

- Confession and Repentance—Always enter your time of prayer with a pure heart. "If we confess our sins, He is faithful and just, and will forgive us our sins and cleanse us from all unrighteousness" (1 John 1:9).

- Thanksgiving and Gratitude—Believers honor God by entering His courts with a grateful heart. "Magnify Him with thanksgiving" (Psalm 69:30).

- Supplication and Prayer—Our requests are presented through intimate conversations with God. "Let your requests be made known to God" (Philippians 4:6).

STEP OF FAITH

We all tend to avoid praying for the impossible, either lacking faith or believing that our problem is too big for the Lord. However, the Word declares, "With God nothing will be impossible" (Luke 1:37).

Take a step of faith by writing down your prayer for the impossible, a prayer that can only be answered by God and God alone.

PROCLAMATION

O Lord of hosts, I come to Your throne in ADORATION, for You are holy and worthy of praise. I CONFESS my sins and repent of them. With THANKSGIVING and gratitude I bring forth my prayer of SUPPLICATION and ask that You hear my cry.

Father—God of Abraham, Isaac, and Jacob—I am seated at Your right hand with Christ my Redeemer because of the exceeding greatness of Your power. I take the authority freely given to me at the moment of my salvation and call forth those things that are not as though they were until they are.

I am a fervent believer in Your Word and will stand my ground against the spirit of fear and doubt that battle against me. And I will wait with all faith and hope for Your supernatural provision.

I am endued as a believer with Your throne power, and I will be victorious! I will wait upon Your answer with all confidence and expectation, for nothing is impossible with You. Amen.

Chapter 6

Sacrifice— Absolute Submission

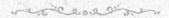

*And now my head shall be lifted up above my enemies
all around me; therefore I will offer sacrifices of joy
in His tabernacle; I will sing, yes,
I will sing praises to the LORD.*

PSALM 27:6

SCRIPTURAL FOUNDATIONS

Read 1 Samuel 1:19–28.

Verse 19: *Then they rose early in the morning and worshiped before the LORD, and returned and came to their house at Ramah. And Elkanah knew Hannah his wife, and the LORD remembered her.*

Elkanah and his family were preparing to leave on their journey back to Ramah. They had attended all the services at the tabernacle of meeting during the celebration of Passover, yet they still "rose early" to honor God before their departure.

The word *worshiped* in this verse means "prostrated," which is the act of lying flat on the ground, face downward, in reverence and total surrender to God. Elkanah and Hannah were signifying their sole reliance on the Lord of hosts. It was because of Hannah's vow and the couple's declaration of dependence on Him for the answer to their prayer that God remembered Hannah.

Verse 20: *So it came to pass in the process of time that Hannah conceived and bore a son, and called his name Samuel, saying, "Because I have asked for him from the LORD."*

God has an appointed time for everything under the sun (Ecclesiastes 3:1–8). There was an appointed time for Isaac's birth (Genesis 21:2), for the festivals of the Lord (Leviticus 23:4)—and God will show His favor upon Zion at a set time (Psalm 103:13). Even though barren Hannah had cried out to the Lord for over nineteen years, the Lord had a distinct timeline for giving her a son. Samuel would not only bless her but influence the nation of Israel.

> *The blessings of God are meaningless unless the recipient has ultimate faith in Him as the Source of all blessings.*

Once Hannah conceived, she undoubtedly declared blessings on her baby every day while he was in her womb. I can imagine the look on her face when she discovered that the baby she had delivered was a boy! Surely her heart pounded with joy as she held her firstborn, a son given to her by the Lord of hosts.

I can hear Elkanah's prayer too, as Samuel is brought into the covenant of Abraham, Isaac, and Jacob on the eighth day of his life: "Blessed art Thou, O LORD our God, King of the universe, who hast sanctified us with Thy commandments, and hast commanded us to make our sons enter the covenant of Abraham our father." After the naming, Elkanah would have continued to pray over Samuel: "May we, in love, continue to give sustenance to this child and provide for his physical needs. May we provide spiritual sustenance through examples of goodness and loving-kindness and by teaching the insights of the Torah and the traditions of our people."[1]

Can you envision the look of jubilation on Hannah's face as she hears these sacred prayers spoken over *her* son? This was the day she had been longing for!

Hannah and Elkanah named their son Samuel, which literally translates "Because I have asked for him from the LORD" (1 Samuel 1:20). In Judaism, naming a child is a profound moment. It is believed that a name calls forth the child's character and divine destiny; it defines one's essence. Samuel's name was a grateful memorial to the goodness and faithfulness of God in the past, and an incentive of hope and faith in the future. Samuel's name, like that of Christ's ("Anointed One of God"), was a constant reminder not only of his destiny but of his duty. Every time Hannah called Samuel's name, it would perpetuate a remembrance of God's favor in answering her prayers. And every time Samuel heard his name called, he would remember the Lord for His grace and mercy.

Verses 21–23: *Now the man Elkanah and all his house went up to offer to the LORD the yearly sacrifice and his vow. But Hannah did not go up, for she said to her husband, "Not until the child is weaned; then I will take him, that he may appear before the LORD and remain there forever." So Elkanah her husband said to her, "Do what seems best to you; wait until you have weaned him. Only let the LORD establish His word." Then the woman stayed and nursed her son until she had weaned him.*

The blessings of God are meaningless unless the recipient has ultimate faith in Him as the Source of all blessings. Both Hannah and Elkanah knew that Samuel's birth was God's direct answer to Hannah's vow. Elkanah was eager to remain faithful to his duty of honoring the festivals of the Lord and also to present the offerings he had vowed in gratitude for Samuel's birth.

> *Both Hannah and Elkanah displayed mutual submission: she to her husband's lead and he to his wife's need.*

Hannah felt it was important to stay behind with her baby—something she could not do without her husband's approval. She desired to keep Samuel in Ramah until he was fully weaned and physically mature enough to be left in the service of the High

Priest. Both Hannah and Elkanah displayed mutual submission: she to her husband's lead and he to his wife's need.

Verses 24–27: *Now when she had weaned him, she took him up with her, with three bulls, one ephah of flour, and a skin of wine, and brought him to the house of the LORD in Shiloh. And the child was young. Then they slaughtered a bull, and brought the child to Eli. And she said, "O my lord! As your soul lives, my lord, I am the woman who stood by you here, praying to the LORD. For this child I prayed, and the LORD has granted me my petition which I asked of Him."*

In biblical times a child was normally weaned at twenty-four months. Samuel, however, was most likely thirty-six months old, for only at that age could children be admitted to the service of the temple (2 Chronicles 31:16).[2]

For Hannah, every day with Samuel had been a blessing, and now she was preparing his belongings for the journey to the tabernacle of meeting. I'm certain her head was filled with questions as they neared Shiloh: *Who will make sure Samuel eats well? Who will put him to bed at night? Lord, who will hold him in their arms and comfort him when he cries out for me? Will he witness the immoral behavior going on in Shiloh? Who will protect my Samuel from evil?*

Samuel's parents arrived in Shiloh ready to make a thanksgiving offering to the Lord before submitting their young son for a lifetime of religious service. Hannah testified to the High Priest of her answered prayer, and then she was prepared to fulfill her promise. She did, though, have a very special request: she asked Eli to supervise her little boy's upbringing. Ordinarily a Levite began service in the temple at the age of twenty-five, but Samuel was only three; she wanted Eli's assurance that he would care for her young son.

Verse 28: "*Therefore I also have lent him to the* LORD; *as long as he lives he shall be lent to the* LORD. *" So they worshiped the* LORD *there.*

Hannah had made an irrevocable vow to the Lord. So why did she use the word *lent* when she surrendered Samuel to Him? God had given Samuel to her, and in turn Hannah would present her son to Him as her ultimate act of submission in thanks for her answered petition. I will elaborate later in our study about Hannah "lending" Samuel to God.

LIFE APPLICATION

But as for me and my house, we will serve the Lord.
JOSHUA 24:15

I have thought long and hard on Hannah's submitting Samuel to the Lord's work at such a young age. No matter how noble it sounds, I find it difficult to wrap my head around such an unimaginable act of surrender. But that is exactly what sets Hannah apart from other women. That is why God chose her to be the mother of one of the greatest prophets of all time.

Hannah had devoted herself to her baby boy for three short years. Imagine her holding Samuel close to her breast as she stared down at his beautiful face. See his tiny finger embracing her own, revealing the remarkable bond between mother and son that was set in place for a lifetime. Certainly the thought crossed her mind, *Why couldn't it be a while longer before our time of separation?*

Hannah easily could have rationalized why it was not good to give her young son over to the High Priest. Yes, Eli had led an upright life loyal to God's service, and as far as biblical records show, he had never committed a "positive wrong"; but he also failed to perform an "assertive right."[3] In other words, Eli may not have ever clearly broken the Ten Commandments, but he had one great fault, one fatal flaw: he failed to assert proper parental authority and discipline over his sons. Eli was described as having weak eyes (1 Samuel 3:2)—perhaps because of his naturally failing vision, but also due to his declining spiritual discernment. In other words, he was blind both physically and spiritually.

Who's to say that Eli's sons could not have become moral leaders had their father properly trained and corrected them according to the Word of the Lord? Instead, they and their despicable lifestyle were the very reason that religious practices became detestable to the people of Israel.

Think of what must have been going through Hannah's mind. She had submitted herself in every way to the Lord, and He knew her heart. Wouldn't God understand if she waited until righteousness had returned to Shiloh before leaving her three-year-old son there? Elkanah was an honorable man, a loving husband, and a godly father; why couldn't *he* teach Samuel about the Lord and then send him to serve with Eli in the tabernacle of meeting at the customary Levitical age of twenty-five? However, Hannah *knew what she meant* when she presented her vow to God that day in Shiloh. To do anything else would have been justifying herself away from her promise; therefore, she faithfully offered her son.

After being absent from the central sanctuary of Israel for three years, Hannah now arrives once more at its entrance. Standing on the well-remembered spot where she had prayed in her distress, she fulfills her vow and lends back to God the sacred treasure entrusted to her care. She will leave Samuel's belongings with Eli, which include a linen robe she lovingly made for him to wear while performing his tabernacle duties.

Then Hannah prepares to return to Ramah without her beloved son.

Submission: The Act of Surrender and Obedience

- *What is submission?* To submit means to yield to a higher power or to the authority or will of another person. It is an act of surrender, a self-denial that results from offering ourselves to the Lord and meeting the needs of others. In order to fully comprehend the definition of a word or action, it is often beneficial to understand what it is not. Submission is *not*:
  - ○ Self-pleasing (Read 2 Timothy 3:2; Luke 9:23.)
  - ○ Man-pleasing (Read 1 Thessalonians 2:4.)
  - ○ Loving the things of the world more than loving the things of God (Read 2 Timothy 4:9–10.)
  - ○ Prideful; instead, it is the act of doing what you don't want to do with a pure and joyful heart (Read Jeremiah 9:23–24.)

After you've read the above Scriptures, write down what submission means to you.

....

....

....

....

....

- *Who should we submit to?*
  - To God, our Father (Read James 4:7.)
  - To Christ, our Redeemer (Read 2 Corinthians 10:5.)
  - To the Holy Spirit, our Comforter (Read 1 Peter 1:22.)
  - To our delegated spiritual authority:
    1. Parents (Read Ephesians 6:2–3.)
    2. Spouse (Read 1 Peter 3:1.)
    3. Pastor (Read Hebrews 13:17.)
    4. Elders (Read 1 Peter 5:5.)
  - To one another (Read Ephesians 5:21.)

Write down the names of those you are submitted to and why.

_____

_____

_____

_____

_____

_____

- *Why should we submit?*
  - Because it is God's will. (Read 2 Chronicles 30:8.)
  - Because it brings God's blessings. (Read Deuteronomy 28:1–3.)
  - Because God gives grace to the humble, by which we are able to:

1. Forgive our offenders (Read Mark 11:25.)
2. Reconcile with others (Read Matthew 5:24.)
3. Satisfy our souls (Read Isaiah 58:11.)
4. Come into the presence of the Lord (Read 1 Thessalonians 2:19)

After reading the suggested Scriptures above, write out why you believe submission is essential to your life.

_____

_____

_____

_____

_____

_____

_____

_____

_____

- *What should we submit?*
  - ○ Our will and affections (Read 1 Peter 4:2.)
  - ○ Our time and talents (Read Joshua 22:5.)
  - ○ Our plans and purposes (Read Proverbs 16:3.)
  - ○ Our pleasures and possessions (Read Proverbs 3:9.)
  - ○ Our cares and concerns (Read 1 Peter 5:7.)[4]

After reading the suggested verses, list what you have offered up to God under each category.

_____

_____

_____

_____

_____

_____

How Can We Submit

The only way any of us can submit to God or to each other is with humility:

> Let our minds, behavior, garb, and whole frame be adorned with humility, it is the most beautiful habit we can wear; this will render obedience and duty easy and pleasant; but, if we are disobedient and proud, God will set Himself to oppose and crush us; for He resists the proud, when He gives grace to the humble.[5]

Humility vs. Pride

Humility is a divine source of harmony, enabling the believer to obey and submit to God. Pride is the Enemy's source of strife, for the proud war against God. There is mutual opposition between the Lord and those who are prideful, but He rejoices in the humble of heart.

God faithfully presents His children with life choices, and when it comes to the topic of pride, the choices are to be humbled or be humiliated. What is the difference between the two?

- Humility is an act of our will; humiliation is an act of God.
- Humility is corrective, while humiliation is disciplinary.
- Humility yields blessings; humiliation brings curses.

There is no escape from making the choice. If we do not humble ourselves before God, we suffer the consequences.[6] We can easily then conclude that the Lord's blessings will only rest on the woman who submits to God's will and to His delegated spiritual authority, who obeys His mandates and resists the spirit of pride by clothing herself in humility.

It is impossible to estimate the power of a righteous woman who acknowledges God in all her ways and who by faith holds on to all His promises. As she proclaims blessings over her loved ones with every prayer offered to the Source of all blessings, she is releasing in them a supernatural, life-changing force that cannot be measured. Her prayers, obedience, and sacrifice produce "a wellspring of life" to her and those she holds dear.

> *It is impossible to estimate the power of a righteous woman who acknowledges God in all her ways and who by faith holds on to all His promises.*

LIFE STORIES

The Righteous Among the Nations

In every era there are individuals who set aside their personal agendas and aspirations to help meet the needs of others as mandated in God's Word. They choose to humble themselves—to give of their time and talents and bravely stand in the gap between right and wrong, good and evil, light and darkness. There is no reward, no ulterior motive, no personal gain; they merely decide to do good in the eyes of the Lord, and their results are supernatural.

The Righteous Among the Nations are the Christians who risked their lives to help Jews during the Holocaust. By acknowledging these individuals, the survivors have sought to honor those who stood against the spirit of apathy, compliance, and collaboration within Nazi Germany. Because of the self-sacrifice of these Christians, the Jews they saved were able to rebuild their lives with a restored faith in humanity.

The Righteous are persons who not only helped the Jews but who risked their lives to *save* Jews. They were willing to stop being mere bystanders and prepared themselves to pay the ultimate price for their righteous cause. They believed that consummate evil required exceptional sacrifice in order to do what was right in the eyes of God.[7] Irena Sendler was one such woman of valor.

Irena

Irena was a twenty-nine-year-old Catholic social worker employed by the Welfare Department of Warsaw at the start of World War II. After the German Occupation, the department continued to take care of deprived and displaced people in the city. Irena used her position to help the Jews, but when the ghetto was sealed off in November 1940, her mission became practically impossible.

Nearly four hundred thousand Jews were ruthlessly driven into a small area assigned to the ghetto, and their situation quickly deteriorated. Appalling unsanitary living conditions, starvation, and lack of medical supplies caused the rampant spread of disease, which led to exorbitantly high death rates. In spite of great personal danger, Irena devised a way into the desperately overcrowded ghetto and began to help the dying Jews by smuggling out as many as she could and arranging hiding places for them.

After the Nazis deported 280,000 Jews from Warsaw to the Treblinka concentration camp in the fall of 1942, Irena became an activist with the newly formed Council for Aid to Jews (Zegota). By this time, most of the Jews in Warsaw had been killed. However, the organization played a crucial role in rescuing a large number of those who survived the massive deportations by continuing to find them hiding places and paying for their upkeep and medical care when needed.

In September 1943, four months after the Warsaw ghetto was completely destroyed, Irena was appointed director of Zegota's Department for the Care of Jewish Children. She used her many contacts with orphanages and various Christian institutions in the surrounding areas to save as many Jewish children as possible. Irena was arrested in October 1943 for her sacrificial work but managed to conceal incriminating evidence, such as the coded addresses of children in the care of Zegota as well as large sums of money used to pay those who helped hide Jews.

Once captured, Irena was tortured for information and sentenced to death for crimes against Germany. She was then sent to the infamous Pawiak Prison, where underground activists eventually managed to bribe officials to release her. But Irena's close encounter with death did not deter her from her righteous work of smuggling Jewish children to safety through her underground network. She smuggled the children out of harm's way in suitcases, ambulances, coffins, sewer pipes, rucksacks, and on one occasion, even a toolbox. Those children old enough to ask knew their deliverer only by her code name "Jolanta."[8]

Irena made her life's work the rescue of innocent lives. It is thought that she saved more than 2,500 Jews; yet who is to say what her final impact was, for "whoever saves a life, it is considered as if they saved an entire world."[9]

The Ultimate Sacrifice

When it came to protecting their children and praying for their very survival, there are no greater heroes than the Jewish mothers of the Holocaust. This was a time when the horror of "madness let loose" produced a killing machine designed to wipe God's chosen people off the face of the earth. It was a time unimaginable, unthinkable; a time incomprehensible to *any* mother or to *any* human.

And when I see a Jewish child walking the streets of Jerusalem, I can hear the echoes of these valiant mothers. I sense the unbridled love of women who withstood the evil beast of annihilation with sacrificial courage, absolute conviction, and unparalleled faith. Chaya Lau was such a mother.

Chaya

When the Nazis rounded up the Jews of Piotrekow, Poland, for deportation, four-year-old Yisrael was supposed to accompany his mother, Chaya, to Ravensbruck. Ravensbruck was Himmler's notorious "women's camp" where deaths by starvation, beating, torture, hanging, shooting, and medical experiments were a grotesque part of daily life.

Chaya's husband and eldest son had already been taken to the camp at Treblinka, and she had not seen or heard from them since. Now the frightened mother and her two remaining sons were standing surrounded by trains, machine guns, Nazis, and vicious dogs. Her head was reeling; how could she keep her children together? Suddenly, Chaya's eighteen-year-old son, Naftali, was grouped with the men, and she and little Yisrael were crowded onto a platform ready to be shoved into the freight car designated for women.

Chaya had to think quickly. She had heard that the Nazis would kill children shortly after they arrived at the women's camp. The valiant mother made a decision that ripped her heart from her chest: she pushed her precious Yisrael away, allowing his older brother to quickly hide him in his duffel bag.

Both of Chaya's beloved sons were now bound for Buchenwald, which was considered a "safer" camp. The loving mother prayed that her boys would both have a better chance of survival there than at Ravensbruck.

Naftali smuggled Yisrael into the labor camp since a child his age would have been immediately exterminated if discovered. Yisrael became the youngest and smallest inmate in the camp, and his survival was largely due to his older brother's constant self-sacrifice and protection in fulfilment of a commitment he had made to his parents.

Chaya didn't survive Ravensbruck, but her boys did survive

Buchenwald. Because of her sacrifice and God's supernatural protection, her cherished little one grew up to carry on a thousand-year unbroken chain of rabbis. Because of Chaya's legacy of love and sacrifice, Yisrael Meir Lau became the Chief Rabbi of Israel and one of the most revered Jews in the world.

Rabbi Yisrael remembers the traumatic separation from his mother.

> At the last second before boarding the train, my mother gave me a hard shove over to the men, whom she hoped would be used for labor and not killed.
>
> "Naftali!" she called to my brother. "Take Yisrael! Goodbye, Naftali! Goodbye, Yisrael!" I never saw her again.
>
> There was no time to discuss whether Mama's move was best. All I knew was that I'd been separated from my mother by force, and I took out all my rage on Naftali, hammering on his chest with my little fists. He tried to hold me, to soothe me, but I refused to calm down. I remember how terribly cold I felt all over; that was the cold of November 1944.
>
> The men gave me hot coffee to drink, but I spit it out and cried myself to sleep. Never in my short life had I cried like that, and never in all the long years since then. It took a long time until I understood that by pushing me away, my mother had saved my life.[10]

And *that's* what love looks like . . .

These two stories reflect the sacrificial actions of two women, one Christian and one Jewish. Both were used by God to save a nation.

SPIRITUAL CHECKLIST

1. *Remember, nothing is sanctified by God until it is submitted to Him. Contemplate what you have learned about submission in this chapter and then list the ways you are submitted to the Lord.*

2. *If you are married, are you submitted to your husband? Read
    1 Peter 3:1–6. List the purpose of marital submission according
    to these verses.*

_____

_____

_____

_____

_____

STEP OF FAITH

Let us come before God and repent of our rebellion, and with a
pure heart declare to the Enemy that he has no place in us, for
we have chosen to surrender to the God of Abraham, Isaac, and
Jacob—and Him alone! No matter what our age, position, or life
experiences, we should do what is right before the Lord.

What steps can you take to be more submissive to God's will?

_____

_____

_____

_____

_____

PROCLAMATION

Father, I come before Your throne in the spirit of contrition and ask that You forgive me of the rebellious acts I have committed against You. I surrender my life to You in every way. I will resist the Enemy and submit to You; let Your will be done and not mine. I pledge to throw off my cloak of pride and put on my garment of humility.

I offer up a sacrifice of praise as Your grace and blessings fall on my life. I pledge to submit to those whom You have placed over me, and to do so with a right spirit. I thank You, Lord, for You are my joy for today and my hope for tomorrow. In Your strength I will rely. Amen.

Chapter 7

The Song—
The Power
of Praise

Shout joyfully to the LORD, all the earth;
break forth in song, rejoice, and sing praises.

PSALMS 98:4

SCRIPTURAL FOUNDATIONS

Read 1 Samuel 2:1–10.

Hannah's Song is described by both Jewish and Christian scholars as a beautiful and sincere expression of gratitude. It is recorded as one of history's greatest prophetic songs along with the songs of Moses (Deuteronomy 32:1–43), Miriam (Exodus 15:20–21), Deborah (Judges 5), King David (2 Samuel 22), Elizabeth (Luke 1:41–45), and Mary (Luke 1:46–55), to name a few.

The song opens with personal references and then progressively expands to include the character and acts of God and the glories of the coming Messiah, all the while interweaving images of prophetic events.[1] Much of Hannah's lyrical prose is interpreted as a series of prophecies that reference future miracles of salvation. Thematically, it acknowledges that victory and defeat, prosperity and poverty, dignity and degradation are temporary conditions. The Lord permits each condition according to what His people need at any given time, or what is necessary for the fulfillment of His divine plan. The song also emphasizes that obedience and prayer can effect changes in the life of an individual.[2]

> *Hannah's song emphasizes that obedience and prayer can effect changes in the life of an individual.*

Verse 1: *And Hannah prayed and said: "My heart rejoices in the* LORD; *my horn is exalted in the* LORD. *I smile at my enemies, because I rejoice in Your salvation."*

- "Prayed"—This form of prayer is an expression of praise to God. Hannah "sang" to the ultimate Source of her joy, with jubilant thanksgiving.
- "Horn"—Refers to David's future reign as king of Israel. Hannah's son, Samuel, will one day anoint him with oil poured from a ram's horn.[3] King David's rule will endure

for all time, for his descendant is Jesus Christ, our eternal Redemption.

- "Smile"—The disappointments of the past—Hannah's years of barrenness, Peninnah's scorn, Elkanah's well-meaning but futile attempts at encouragement, Eli's accusation of drunkenness—no longer mattered once God answered her prayer.[4]

Verse 2: *"No one is holy like the LORD, for there is none besides You, nor is there any rock like our God."*

Hannah attributes her joy to God's incomparable holiness. She knows that, outside of God, there is no existence; He is the One who intervened in nature, enabling her barren womb to bear a child.

The word *rock* refers to God as the Source of our strength and protection; He is steadfast in our time of trouble (Psalm 18:2).

Verses 3–4: *"Talk no more so very proudly; let no arrogance come from your mouth, for the LORD is the God of knowledge; and by Him actions are weighed. The bows of the mighty men are broken, and those who stumbled are girded with strength."*

According to biblical scholars, Hannah is now prophetically singing of all the prideful rulers who will speak openly against God and take His people into captivity. But God is all wise and all knowing; His knowledge is immediate, perfect, and universal. He will destroy these men and their kingdoms forever, for Genesis declares that the person or nation that blesses Israel will be blessed, and those who curse Israel will be cursed (12:3).

"Those who stumbled" refers to the weak and helpless whom God will faithfully uphold.

Verse 5: *"Those who were full have hired themselves out for bread, and the hungry have ceased to hunger. Even the barren has borne seven, and she who has many children has become feeble."*

Hannah gives examples of how God will reverse the circumstances of the arrogant and the plight of the humble. Those who consider themselves entitled while ignoring the needs of others will one day find themselves destitute. And those who live without will one day no longer have to struggle.

Hannah endured the haughty glares of the gloating Peninnah as she flaunted her ability to bear children. Hannah witnessed the arrogant sons of Eli living above the laws of God. But through her anointed song, the Spirit of the Lord gave Hannah a glimpse of the future.

Why did Hannah's Song mention *seven* children when she would ultimately have *six*? What did the future hold for Peninnah and Eli?

The number *seven* is a biblical equivalent for "many." Although Hannah bore five more children after Samuel (1 Samuel 2:21), the numerical reference in this verse suggests that Samuel was better than *two* sons. Think of it: Elkanah promised to be better than *ten* sons, and God gave Hannah a son who could bring more joy to her than *two*. Samuel's life accomplishments would equate to more than Hannah would ever imagine.

The genealogy of Adam through the ancestry of Seth was recorded beginning in Genesis 5, and as a result we know that Elkanah had eight sons, and Hannah bore him a total of four sons and two daughters. We can therefore conclude that four sons were from Hannah and four sons from Peninnah (1 Chronicles 6:25–28; 1 Samuel 2:21). One of Elkanah's sons with Peninnah was named Ahimoth, which means "My Brother Is Dead." The word *feeble*, or *bereft*, denotes one who has experienced the loss of children.[5] Therefore, Jewish scholars may conclude that Peninnah would one day suffer the death of a child.

What about Eli? Eli's sons "abhorred the offering of the LORD" (1 Samuel 2:17); they desecrated the tabernacle of meeting and caused sin to run rampant in Shiloh. Their weak-eyed father issued a meager warning, but Hophni and Phinehas refused to repent, and eventually God would bring severe punishment upon the house of Eli.

Verse 6: *"The LORD kills and makes alive; He brings down to the grave and brings up."*

This verse is literal. The key to life is in God's hand: He gives life and He takes it (Job 1:21), and He has the power to extend it (2 Kings 20:6) and to resurrect it (2 Kings 4:32–36; Mark 5:35–43; John 11:38–44).

Verses 7–8: *"The LORD makes poor and makes rich; He brings low and lifts up. He raises the poor from the dust, and lifts the beggar from the ash heap, to set them among princes and make them inherit the throne of glory. For the pillars of the earth are the LORD's, and He has set the world upon them."*

Moses commanded the Israelites to remember that it is God who gives His people the power to get wealth (Deuteronomy 8:17–18), and King David would later exalt the Lord for raising "the poor out of the dust" and lifting "the needy out of the ash heap" (Psalm 113:7). Furthermore, this verse is a prophetic utterance concerning the reign of King David and his descendants, which includes the coming Messiah.

Remember, there was no king in Israel during this time, and the ruling High Priest was allowing corruption to run amok.

Additionally, the Philistines were the ever-present enemy (Genesis 21:32; Judges 16:21–30; 1 Samuel 4:10–11; 31:3–6). How could Hannah sing of a "throne" if not for God's Spirit giving her a vision of the coming glory of His kingdom (Job 36:7b; Psalm 113:8)? She was calling those things that were not as though they were.

The verse concludes with the reminder that God, the Architect of the ages, placed the earth on its eternal foundations. His strength will prevail, His enemies will be destroyed, and the Lord's anointed will be empowered.

Verses 9–10: *"He will guard the feet of His saints, but the wicked shall be silent in darkness. For by strength no man shall prevail. The adversaries of the* LORD *shall be broken in pieces; from heaven He will thunder against them. The* LORD *will judge the ends of the earth. He will give strength to His king, and exalt the horn of His anointed."*

The "feet of His saints" refers to the devout ones who obey God's Word. This portion of Hannah's Song once again magnifies the goodness of God that promises to guide the righteous onto a divine path (Psalm 37:23–24; 17:5). God assures His people that He will supernaturally protect them (Psalm 61:3–4), secure the ground they stand on (Isaiah 28:16), establish their going in and coming out (Psalm 121:8), and set His guards of grace and mercy upon them (Psalm 23:6) so that they will not stumble or wander in the way (Psalm 119:165).

The "wicked" of verse 9 and the "adversaries" of verse 10 not only refer to Hannah's accusers and any present and future enemies of Israel's or Samuel's, but to all who come against the Lord of hosts. No form of power, eloquence, or influence will aid God's enemies from escaping the "darkness" of His righteous judgment (Psalm 33:16–22; Matthew 8:12; 22:12–13).

> *Hannah may have uttered*
> *her supplication in silence, but she publicly*
> *proclaimed her praise in song*
> *through the language of her faith in God.*

The last word of Hannah's Song is the first mention of God's anointed. The Hebrew word for "anointed" is *mashiach* and refers to a consecrated person, such as a king or priest, but it is most commonly associated with the coming Messiah. Think of it: Hannah was the first person on earth to ever address God as the "LORD of hosts," and now she was the first to refer to our coming King as His "anointed." After her song, prophets like Samuel (2 Samuel 2:35), David (Psalm 2:2; 45:7), Isaiah (Isaiah 61:1), and Daniel (Daniel 9:25–26) were given visions of the Messiah. And most importantly, when Jesus walked the earth, many of those who knew Him called Him the Anointed One (John 1:41; 4:25).

Hannah may have uttered her supplication in silence, but she publicly proclaimed her praise in song through the language of her faith in God.

LIFE APPLICATION

> *The steadfast of mind You will keep in perfect peace,*
> *because he trusts in You. Trust in the LORD forever,*
> *for in God the LORD, we have an everlasting Rock.*
> ISAIAH 26:3–4 NASB

The whole of Hannah's song is focused on the Lord of hosts, on His mercy, His grace, and His strength. We live hectic lives full of daily responsibilities and challenges, yet we must set our minds on God in order to live in victory.

Read the Song of Praise for God's Favor in Isaiah 25 and the Song of Trust for His Protection in Isaiah 26. Write down how believers can focus on God and His goodness.

_____

_____

_____

_____

_____

_____

_____

Even though Hannah was tormented by Peninnah's cruelty, there is no record that she judged or mistreated Peninnah for her unkind actions. The only reference to Peninnah after Samuel's birth is within the lyrics of this song. Hannah's attitude toward her was a testimony that God is only concerned with what we as His children do right, not with what others do wrong. Peninnah, like all of us, would one day answer to the Judge of all judges.

Do not rejoice when your enemy falls,
And do not let your heart be glad when he stumbles;
Lest the LORD see it, and it displease Him,
And He turn away His wrath from him.
Do not fret because of evildoers, nor be envious of the wicked;
For there will be no prospect for the evil man;
The lamp of the wicked will be put out. (Proverbs 24:17–20)

But I say to you, love your enemies, bless those who curse you, do good to those who hate you, and pray for those who spitefully use you and persecute you. (Matthew 5:44)

It is our duty to show our adversaries the love of God, just as He displayed His unconditional love for us. Our love for others is our testament that Christ lives in us.

Read Matthew 5:43–48 and Jude 1:21. List those who have offended you, then write down their offense. Next, pray and make a conscious decision to forgive them, remembering their offense no more. Finally, speak blessings over them. This very personal and private exercise will bring you supernatural freedom from the effects of others' insults or actions.

The Lord displays His unconditional love to us in so many ways. *Using your Bible's concordance look up Scriptures that reflect God's love in the selections below and write down the one that is the most meaningful to you.*[6]

Mercy is God's forgiving love. ....

Grace is God's undeserving love. ....

Kindness is God's caring love. ....

Christ's death is God's proven love. ....

God's will is God's unerring love. ....

Heaven is God's rewarding love. ....

Eternity is God's unending love. ....

LIFE STORIES

The best illustrations of life stories for this chapter are two from among the several women in Scripture whose songs reflect the reward of their obedience and sacrifice.

Miriam

The first is Miriam, the daughter of Amram and Jochebed and the elder sister of Aaron and Moses. Her Hebrew name means "Bitterness and Rebellious,"[7] for in the time of her birth, the people of Israel experienced the cruelest phase of Egyptian oppression. Later in life, Miriam would question God's anointing of Moses and suffer the consequence of her insubordinate actions (Numbers 12:1–15).

According to certain rabbinic teachings, Caleb—a descendant from Judah—married Miriam and fathered Hur. Hur was Moses and Aaron's nephew (1 Chronicles 2:19).[8] This is the same Hur who, along with Aaron, later supported Moses's arms in Israel's battle against the Amalekites (Exodus 17:11–13).[9]

Miriam's family and the Israelites in Egyptian captivity suffered the persecution of Pharaoh and his evil decrees. All the children born at the time of Moses's birth were under a death sentence. In a desperate desire to save her son's life, Moses's mother placed her three-month-old infant in a pitch-lined basket on the banks of the Nile. She then assigned seven-year-old Miriam to "watch from afar" as he floated down the great river (Exodus 2:4).

Think of the heavy yoke of responsibility Miriam carried as she watched over the innocent life in the wicker basket. Yet she remained faithful to her mission and never took her eyes off the small bundle. Little did Miriam realize that she was escorting her baby brother to his divine destiny.

Imagine Miriam anxiously following close behind the makeshift ark as it rolled down the huge river. Questions reeled through her mind: *Will the waters swallow Moses into the deep? Will the vicious Nile crocodiles devour him? Where will the winding river take my baby brother?*

Providentially, Pharaoh's daughter Bilhah (1 Chronicles 4:18)[10] is bathing in the Nile. She sees the basket and orders her maidservant to salvage the baby from the murky waters. Instantly Miriam appears from the dense brush and courageously approaches one of the most powerful women on earth to suggest that a Hebrew nursemaid tend to the infant for a season. The princess agrees, and by nightfall, Miriam takes Moses back to their ever-grateful mother, who is able to care for him until he is fully weaned.

Nothing in Scripture is happenstance. Within the God-inspired actions of Jochebed and Miriam and the compassion of Bilhah lay the defeat of Satan, the preservation of a nation, the fulfillment of prophecy, and the furtherance of God's plan concerning the coming Seed of the woman (Genesis 3:15) that would ultimately redeem mankind.[11]

Every player in this supernatural rescue was divinely directed by the Lord of hosts, even Bilhah's maidservant. One of the Hebrew meanings of the word *maidservant* is "arm." Rabbinical scholars teach that God miraculously extended the arm of the maidservant as far as it needed to go to redeem Moses from the murky waters of the Nile (Exodus 6:6).

This imagery demonstrates that no matter how difficult a righteous act might be, nothing is impossible with the help of God. Judaism further teaches that once a person is redeemed, it is his or her obligation to redeem others—an assignment that Moses would later fulfill.

No matter how difficult a righteous act might be, nothing is impossible with the help of God.

Miriam was the first woman recognized as a prophetess in Scripture (Exodus 15). She was known as a woman of courage, one who could think quickly and take decisive action. Therefore, we can appreciate why God chose her to stand by Moses and Aaron eighty years later as they led Israel out of Egypt in the massive and seemingly impossible mission of the exodus through the Red Sea (Micah 6:4).

After the Lord miraculously redeemed His children by parting the sea, and after He consumed Pharaoh's army under the very same waters, He used Miriam to help Moses lead the Israelites in song as they declared their praise to the God of Abraham, Isaac, and Jacob.

The Song of Moses was composed by Moses and sung by all of Israel. It consisted of three distinctly marked parts beginning with praise to Jehovah and ending with the promise of God eternally reigning over His enemies (Exodus 15:1–19). Moses led the men, and Miriam led the women with timbrels and dance, singing the refrain of exhortation: "Sing to the LORD, for He has triumphed gloriously! The horse and its rider He has thrown into the sea!" (Exodus 15:21).

Miriam and her chorus of women delivered the Song of Moses with an intensity of feeling and a depth of faith unique to all women. The women of Israel had wailed uncontrollably as their infant sons were executed at birth or sacrificed in the Nile (Exodus 1:16, 22). They had suffered anguish as their husbands and sons needlessly labored under the increasingly harsh Egyptian rule (Exodus 5). Yet their faith in God endured and grew stronger as they waited for His redemption.

Miriam instilled in these women a God-centered trust in the future, allowing them to rise above the despair of the present. Therefore, once redeemed, their joy was exponentially multiplied, for they had hope that never again in their lifetime would they see their husbands and children suffer at the hand of an oppressor.

Miriam, along with her two brothers, provided the Jewish people with the elements necessary for redemption. All three led in their unique way: Moses taught the Torah, Aaron led through his service as the High Priest, and Miriam by leading and teaching the women.[12]

Miriam left a legacy for all Israel. She taught the women to rise above the darkness with the light of hope. She infused in them a steadfast faith in the One True God who would ensure their future in the midst of hardship and pain. Through her insight and firm convictions, Miriam encouraged the women to fulfill their divine mission, bringing about the very survival of a people and a nation.

Both Hannah and Miriam suffered the pangs of separation as one returned her beloved brother to Pharaoh's household and the other submitted her long-awaited son to the service of the Lord in Shiloh. *Both* had to trust God. *Both* had faith that He was in control. *Both* believed that God's divine plan would be fulfilled. *Both* left a legacy for others to follow. And *both* women expressed their joy and gratitude to the Lord in heartfelt song.

Mary

The second woman was Mary. She was the daughter of Eli from the tribe of Judah and of the lineage of David (Luke 3:23–38). Her name is the Greek transliteration of the Hebrew name Miriam, which means "Bitterness," as we learned above. However, in Aramaic—which was the spoken language of the time—it means "Blessed and Strength."[13]

The Scriptures reveal quite a bit about Mary's life. Among her relatives were Zacharias and Elizabeth (Luke 1:36). Her husband was Joseph, who was also a descendant of the house of David

(Luke 2:4). After Mary accomplished her divine assignment, she and Joseph had four sons.[14] We know that before her union with Joseph, and six months after the miraculous conception of Elizabeth's son, John, Mary received a visitor—an angelic messenger from God named Gabriel (Luke 1:26).

The angel gave to this young virgin a prophetic revelation of her firstborn son. Several prophets had previously mentioned Him in the Torah. Centuries before, the prophet Micah had declared His coming birth in Bethlehem (Micah 5:2). Isaiah referred to a child born of a virgin who would be called Immanuel, "God with us" (Isaiah 7:14). And Jeremiah proclaimed He would be a king who would reign in righteousness (Jeremiah 23:5). Little did Mary know that she would play a vital part in what they foretold.

The gospel of Luke clearly documents Mary's exchange with Gabriel; she asked only *one* question, and then with blind faith, submitted to God's will even though she did not understand how the prophecy could possibly come to pass. Soon after, Mary went to Judah and shared her extraordinary news with her cousin Elizabeth. Mary was so infused with the presence of God that when she entered the house of Zacharias, the baby Elizabeth was carrying leapt within her. Elizabeth was instantly filled with the Holy Spirit, and she too began to prophesy about Mary's forthcoming son (Luke 1:41–45).

It is at this time that Mary sang her song:

My soul magnifies the Lord,
And my spirit has rejoiced in God my Savior.
For He has regarded the lowly state of His maidservant;
For behold, henceforth all generations will call me blessed.

For He who is mighty has done great things for me,
And holy is His name.
And His mercy is on those who fear Him
From generation to generation.
He has shown strength with His arm;
He has scattered the proud in the imagination of their hearts.
He has put down the mighty from their thrones,
And exalted the lowly.
He has filled the hungry with good things,
And the rich He has sent away empty.
He has helped His servant Israel,
In remembrance of His mercy,
As He spoke to our fathers,
To Abraham and to his seed forever. (Luke 1:46–55)

Mary's Song is also known as "The Magnificat," which in Latin means "My soul magnifies." Mary's melody beautifully expresses adoration and praise for the Lord of hosts, who bestowed His grace and favor upon her life.

Within its verses Mary refers to herself as "blessed." There are two Greek forms of this word; the first carries the meaning "indwelt by God." Mary was declaring that she would be remembered by generations to come as one who carried within her the Spirit of the Living God. The second form has a broader meaning, "indwelt by God and therefore fully satisfied," which asserts that God's presence will produce in the believer a supernatural peace and fulfillment no matter what the circumstances may be.[15]

God's words are God's promises. Mary was trusted by the Lord of hosts not only to participate in and witness marvelous miracles but to endure severe hardships. Scripture chronicles some of her joys and sorrows: She withstood the ridicule of inquiring minds concerning her untimely pregnancy (Matthew 1:19). She gave birth to the prophesied Child under harsh conditions (Luke 2:7). Joseph and Mary dutifully dedicated Him in the temple in Jerusalem and called His name Jesus (Luke 2:21–22), and shortly thereafter the young family was forced to flee Judah to escape Herod's persecution (Matthew 2:13–15). Later, Mary and Joseph humbly witnessed Jesus in the temple at the age of thirteen (fully twelve), discussing Torah with learned scholars (Luke 2:46). Oh, how Mary must have treasured her time with her precious Gift from above (Luke 2:51)! She even watched her Son lovingly minister to people with His miracle-working powers as she and His disciples traveled with Jesus from town to town (John 2:1–9, 12).

And then it happened: the tide of public opinion over her Son's good works turned. Mary watched in disbelief and anguish as He was falsely accused, tried, sentenced to death, and tortured. And finally, this woman who was favored and blessed of God watched in agony as Jesus suffered a most horrifying death by crucifixion.

Mary was told that Joseph of Arimathea and Nicodemus had prepared her Son's body for burial and then hurriedly placed Jesus in a nearby sepulcher before the beginning of the Sabbath. And now she was readying her home for *Shiva*.[16] Mary lit the candle that would remain lit for seven days and received her remaining children, their immediate families, and His disciples for a time of mourning.

There she sat, oblivious to the cries of the other mourners as she recalled God's many promises given through the angel Gabriel, her cousin Elizabeth, and the righteous Simeon and the prophetess Anna (Luke 2:25–38). I can only imagine the questions that flooded her mind: *What of my Son's reign over the house of David? What about Jesus being the fulfillment of God's Word? Simeon and Anna said my Son would be the glory of God's people and the redemption of Jerusalem, but Jesus is dead! What happened?*

The word *blessed* must have kept ringing in Mary's ears. She had watched her precious Son take His last agonizing breath and held His lifeless, bruised, and bloody body on her lap . . . How could she be called *blessed*?

Mary sat *Shiva* for two full days in inconsolable grief. But remember, God's words are God's promises.

On Sunday, the morning of the third day after His death, a woman came rushing into Mary's house and announced that the massive stone of the borrowed tomb had been rolled away and Jesus was gone! Suddenly Mary remembered the words her Son spoke to His disciples: "The Son of Man must be delivered into the hands of sinful men, and be crucified, and the third day rise again" (Luke 24:7).

Mary knew then it would be well with her soul, for the God of Abraham, Isaac, and Jacob would fulfill His Word just as He promised.

God's words are God's promises.

Several people saw Jesus again before His ascension to the Father in heaven, and I'm sure Mary was one of them. Her joy must have been indescribable as she saw her Son—*the* Son—in His resurrected state. It is recorded that Mary later participated in the prayer meeting held in an upper room in Jerusalem during the Feast of Pentecost—and what a prayer meeting it was! Read Paul's account of that life-changing day:

> And suddenly there came a sound from heaven, as of a rushing mighty wind, and it filled the whole house where they were sitting. Then there appeared to them divided tongues, as of fire, and one sat upon each of them. And they were all filled with the Holy Spirit and began to speak with other tongues, as the Spirit gave them utterance. (Acts 2:2–4)

Now I ask you, who could better recognize this Spirit than Jesus's mother? What unrivaled peace she must have felt when the Comforter made residence in her soul! Once and for all time, the manifestations of the prophecies about her Son were made clear to her.

Think on this: a mortal woman became the mother of God, chosen to be an integral part of the glorious work of redemption. We must never worship Mary, but we should always remember her willingness to be used of the Almighty to accomplish His divine plan, no matter how impossible. Bishop T. D. Jakes has said that Mary was distinguished above all women in the courts of man and heaven as the only one to have carried Jesus twice—once in her womb and once in her spirit.

The Songs of Hannah and Mary

The Song of Hannah and the Magnificat have long been compared. Hannah's Song is believed by many to be the seed that helped spring forth the Song of Mary. Even though the songs are 1,100 years apart, and Hannah expressed herself in Hebrew while Mary sang in Aramaic, there still are remarkable parallels between the two. The following are some of their similarities, a true testimony of the inerrancy[17] of God's Word.

- Hannah: "My heart rejoices in the LORD" (1 Samuel 2:1).
- Mary: "My soul glorifies the Lord" (Luke 1:46).

- Hannah: "Because I rejoice in Your deliverance" (1 Samuel 2:1).
- Mary: "My spirit has rejoiced in God my Savior" (Luke 1:47).

- Hannah: "No one is holy like the LORD" (1 Samuel 2:2).
- Mary: "Holy is His name" (Luke 1:49).

- Hannah: "Those who were full have hired themselves out for bread, and the hungry have ceased to hunger" (1 Samuel 2:5).
- Mary: "He has filled the hungry with good things, and the rich He has sent away empty" (Luke 1:53).

- Hannah: "The LORD makes poor and makes rich; He brings low and lifts up. He raises the poor from the dust and lifts the beggar from the ash heap, to set them among princes and make them inherit the throne of glory" (1 Samuel 2:7–8).

- Mary: "He has put down the mighty from their thrones, and exalted the lowly" (Luke 1:52).

- Hannah: "The adversaries of the LORD shall be broken in pieces" (1 Samuel 2:10).
- Mary: "He has scattered the proud" (Luke 1:51).

It is obvious that Mary identified herself with this noble woman named Hannah. The main difference between their extraordinarily similar songs is that one conveys the promise and the other testifies of the *realization* of the promise. The themes uniting the two are God's grace and His sovereign intervention in Israel's history and people to work His will and achieve His victory. Ultimately, that victory *is Christ*, to whom Hannah and Mary, in their unique ways, bear witness.[18]

Both Hannah and Mary were God's chosen vessels. *Both* submitted to their divine assignment. *Both* endured hardship. *Both* their sons were anointed by the Lord of hosts to be a judge and a prophet. But only *One* was destined to become the Savior of the world.

୧୨

Stitch by stitch, you can see this intricate quilt piece together: Miriam's role in the deliverance of Moses, Hannah's vow to offer Samuel for God's service, and Mary's willingness to bring our Savior into the world. All were lovingly woven in place by the Father of creation for the ultimate redemption of mankind.

And *that's* what love looks like.

SPIRITUAL CHECKLIST

Are you singing the wrong song? Miriam, Hannah, and Mary sang praises to the Lord. Are you?

1. *The Song of Criticism.* Read Mark 14:5 and 1 Corinthians 1:10–12. The spirit of murmuring is divisive and unproductive. We often waste our lives complaining about our circumstances instead of thanking God for the many blessings He has afforded us.

    Read Exodus 15:2; Deuteronomy 10:21; 2 Samuel 22:4; Psalm 7:17; 9:1; Luke 19:37; Hebrews 3:15; 1 Peter 2:9. Exchange the Song of Criticism with the Song of Praise by confessing those things you are critical about. Ask God to forgive you and commit to separating yourself from this contentious spirit by praising the Lord for His goodness.

2. *The Song of Despair.* Read Proverbs 12:25 and 2 Corinthians 1:8. Despair and depression are dark spirits that constantly pursue every believer. When faced with a problem, we often fall into the pit of despondency. Yet we can make a choice to climb out of that misery by replacing the Song of Despair with the Song of Joy. *Begin by reading the following psalms out loud: 5:11; 16:11; 27:6; 30:5; 32:11; 35:9, 27; 51:8; 63:5; 98:4; 113:9; 126:5. List those things that you are joyful about.*

_____

_____

_____

_____

_____

_____

_____

_____

_____

3. *The Song of Doubt.* The Scriptures urge us to walk in faith, "doubting nothing" (Acts 10:20; 11:12). Doubt overthrows hope, and hope is the life cord that connects us to our Creator. The songs of King David repeatedly encourage hope in God

(Psalm 42:5, 11; 43:5; 78:7), and Jesus told His disciples in Mark 11:22 to "have faith in God." Read Romans 11:14, 14:22; Galatians 3:11; Hebrews 11:1–12.

Remember, faith is the bird that feels the light and sings to greet the dawn while it is still dark.[19] Trade your Song of Doubt for the Song of Faith and Hope, and dispel your worries by declaring your trust in God. *Search the Scriptures and list all those having to do with hope and faith in God. Read them daily to bring encouragement to your heart, soul, and mind.*

STEP OF FAITH

Joy was the harvest of Hannah's faith. She planted its seed by choosing to trust God and obey His precepts. She believed that He would not fail her. Once the Lord answered her prayer, she was faithful to keep her vow and present Him with a sacrifice of praise. In return, she bathed in the light of His glory. Remember this truth: the path to joy is always under construction.

What step can you personally take to help develop your trust in God? Make a pledge to daily build on this step by praising Him for the good things He has done, is doing, and will do in your life.

PROCLAMATION

Father—God of Abraham, Isaac, and Jacob—You are good, and Your mercies endure forever. I sing praises to Your holy Name, for You sacrificed Your only Son so I could be redeemed from my sins. You are my Healer, my Provider, my Deliverer, and my Comforter. You are the source of my peace, my joy, my hope. You are the great Promise Keeper of all promise keepers, and because You love me, no good thing will You withhold from me.

Lord of hosts, You hear my cry in the night and bring me joy in the morning. You guide my steps and keep my feet on the divine path that You have created for my life. I will not fear, for You walk beside me and assign Your angels to be my rear guard to protect me from the Evil One.

I stand before You with total praise on my lips and heart because You are faithful to fulfill Your infallible Word in my life and the lives of my loved ones. Amen.

Chapter 8

Supernatural Favor— Abiding in His Blessings

"Hear [Shema], O Israel: The LORD our God, the LORD is one!
You shall love the LORD your God with all your heart,
with all your soul, and with all your strength."

DEUTERONOMY 6:4–5

SCRIPTURAL FOUNDATIONS

Read 1 Samuel 2:11, 18–26.

Verse 11: *Then Elkanah went to his house at Ramah. But the child ministered to the LORD before Eli the priest.*

We have described Hannah's leaving young Samuel in Shiloh, but what about Elkanah? He too was parting from his son; he too was returning home with concerns over Samuel's well-being. Elkanah, like Hannah, was confident that Samuel would fulfill his mother's vow and serve the Lord all his life, but the pain of separation from their son was still great. Faithful Elkanah returned to Ramah and to his Levitical duties, intent on continuing to serve the Lord.

Verse 18: *But Samuel ministered before the* Lord, *even as a child, wearing a linen ephod.*

Samuel's service to the Lord at such a young age is emphasized once more. The word *but* in verses 11 and 18 illustrates the dissimilarity between Samuel's moral fiber and the hideous behavior of Eli's sons. Hophni and Phineas were self-indulgent, putting their carnal desires above others, while Samuel devoted himself unselfishly to the service of God.[1]

Verse 19: *Moreover his mother used to make him a little robe, and bring it to him year by year when she came up with her husband to offer the yearly sacrifice.*

A linen robe was required attire for those who exhibited divinely inspired prophetic expression. The Talmud states, "While [priests] are clothed in the priestly garments, they are clothed in the priesthood; but when they are not wearing the garments, the priesthood is not upon them"[2] (Exodus 28:1–4). Although the robes were worn only by adults, Hannah fashioned small ones for the very young Samuel as a show of affection but also to symbolize her vow that her son would devote his adult life to God as well.[3]

Undoubtedly she prayed for Samuel as she painstakingly made every intricate stitch. Both parents looked forward to their visits with him in Shiloh, but what further joy Hannah must have felt when she lovingly presented Samuel with his new garments of service!

Verse 20: *And Eli would bless Elkanah and his wife, and say, "The Lord give you descendants from this woman for the loan that was given to the Lord." Then they would go to their own home.*

Eli valued Samuel as a gift the more he watched the boy grow in the Lord. In appreciation for these parents bestowing their very young child to religious services, the High Priest blessed Elkanah and Hannah every time they came to worship in the tabernacle of meeting.

The meaning of the Hebrew term *loan* is multifold. In this verse, it refers to the actual presenting of the child to the Lord of hosts; second, it conveys the understanding that Samuel was given both to Hannah *and* to Jehovah. Hannah had not simply asked for a child, but for a son whom she might dedicate to God. And for that sacrifice, Eli now prayed that Jehovah would grant added favor by giving Hannah more children to raise.[4]

> Loan *conveys the understanding that Samuel was given both to Hannah and to Jehovah. Hannah had not simply asked for a child, but for a son whom she might dedicate to God.*

Verse 21a: *And the Lord visited Hannah, so that she conceived and bore three sons and two daughters.*

This verse confirms the manifestation of the High Priest's blessing. Elkanah and Hannah went home confident that Eli's words would be fulfilled—and their confidence proved well directed, because God indeed remembered Hannah with additional offspring.[5]

Verse 21b: *Meanwhile the child Samuel grew before [with] the LORD.*

The Hebrew word *with* implies a close relationship. It is the same word used in the final marriage blessing in Jewish wedding ceremonies, which concludes with the phrase "who gladdens the groom *with* the bride" (emphasis added).[6] The use of this word signifies that the wedding ceremony is complete. Saying that Samuel grew up *with* God not only refers to the degree of his spiritual growth but to the intimate relationship Samuel had with the Lord of hosts.[7] Eli may have had knowledge of God's precepts, but he did not possess Samuel's deep-rooted relationship with God. This lack of sensitivity to God's purposes was evidenced in Eli's weak leadership.

Verses 22–25: *Now Eli was very old; and he heard everything his sons did to all Israel, and how they lay with the women who assembled at the door of the tabernacle of meeting. So he said to them, "Why do you do such things? For I hear of your evil dealings from all the people. No, my sons! For it is not a good report that I hear. You make the LORD's people transgress. If one man sins against another, God will judge him. But if a man sins against the LORD, who will intercede for him?" Nevertheless they did not heed the voice of their father, because the LORD desired to kill them.*

After contrasting the spiritual growth of Samuel with the spiritual decline of Eli, Scripture begins to record the High Priest's tragic end-story. The term *very old* implies that Hophni's and

Phinehas's offenses began after Eli was no longer able to fully function as the High Priest. Tragically, this should have been a time when Eli's sons rose up to carry on their father's legacy of service to God. Instead, they chose to desecrate it.

When Eli addressed his sons' actions, he stated, "I hear of your evil doings from all the people." "All the people" implies common knowledge. Why didn't Eli know *firsthand* of Hophni's and Phinehas's repulsive behavior? Why didn't he address their evil deeds before their conduct became known to the multitudes of Shiloh? Because Eli chose to turn his back on what his sons were doing instead of dismissing them of their priestly duties.

The phrase "not a good report" suggests that the only reason Eli chose to speak out at this time was because his congregants were protesting the detestable actions of these two men. Eli may have indeed chastised his sons with wise words, but they were to no avail; his admonition was weak at best, and certainly not sufficient to restrain their sinful behavior.[8]

Eli should have immediately disciplined his sons by removing them from their tabernacle duties. Instead, his mistake as a father, judge, and High Priest was that he showed excessive tolerance and leniency, making his words of reprimand ineffectual.

1 Samuel 2:27–36 describes a visit from "a man of God." Some Jewish scholars believe this unknown prophet to be Elkanah, Samuel's father. Elkanah not only witnessed the shameful events in Shiloh with his own eyes; he also met the qualifications of a prophet. Elkanah was a prominent Levite in Ramah. He knew the Scriptures, he was pure in his obedience and service to the Lord, he was inspired by the Holy Spirit, and the Lord trusted him with His presence and His message.[9]

The prophet asked Eli on God's behalf, "Why do you kick

at My sacrifice and My offering which I have commanded in
My dwelling place, and honor your sons more than Me . . . ?"
(1 Samuel 2:29).

You have heard it said many times before: "When God asks a
question, it's not because He doesn't know the answer." The Lord
of hosts was very aware of the sins of Hophni and Phineas, but He
had extended Eli the benefit of time to rebuke his sons. This is yet
another display of God's unmerited grace toward all sinners, un-
derscoring the opportunity He affords His own children to repent
and turn away from wrongdoing, thereby avoiding sure judgment.

When Eli's parental reprimand finally came, it was both weak
and futile; therefore, the Lord informed Eli (through His chosen
prophet) that He considered the father a partner in his sons' mis-
deeds. No matter how pious Eli had been in his previous service,
he was now giving greater honor to Hophni and Phineas than
to God. Eli's disloyalty and his feeble attempt at correcting his
sons were so contemptible to God that He would see to it that Eli
would share in their judgment.

The prophet's stern message continued: Eli was told that both
of his sons would die on the same day, and finally, that the priesthood would pass from his house to that of another. This was part
of the same prophecy that was repeated in Samuel's first divine
revelation, which he received while he was still very young.

Verse 26: *And the child Samuel grew in stature, and in favor
both with the Lord and men.*

Unlike Eli's sons, the young Samuel continuously "grew"
in virtue and reputation, even though he lived in the declining
environment at Shiloh's temple. He strictly observed God's law
and considered how his example would affect the lives of others.

Samuel chose to faithfully serve God and set an honorable standard before the people of Israel. Samuel's upstanding way of life enabled him to eventually lead Israel out of darkness and onto the path of repentance and righteousness.[10]

Samuel walked in the favor of God.

> *God's favor is a result of His sovereign mercy and grace; it can manifest through His response to our prayers or as a reward for righteous living.*

LIFE APPLICATION

His name shall endure forever; His name shall continue as long as the sun. And men shall be blessed in Him; all nations shall call Him blessed.

PSALM 72:17

To receive favor is to gain approval, acceptance, and blessings. God's favor is a result of His sovereign mercy and grace; it can manifest through His response to our prayers or as a reward for righteous living.

Noah and Moses walked blameless before the Lord, and they received His favor and honor (Genesis 6:8; Exodus 33:12–13; Psalm 84:11). Joseph's power and prosperity were a result of God's favor (Deuteronomy 33:16). The Scriptures record that Mary "found favor with God" (Luke 1:30), and that both Samuel (1 Samuel 2:26) and Jesus Christ (Luke 2:52) increased in stature and in favor with God. To walk in this favor is to abide in the Lord's blessings. Psalm 72:17 proclaims that "men shall be blessed in Him." The prince of preachers, Charles Haddon Spurgeon, said the following of this scripture:

> If one had the tongues of men and of angels, and if one could only for once use that speech which it is not lawful for a man to utter—those words which Paul tells us that he heard when he was caught up to the third heaven—if we could even speak as never man yet spake, we could not fully set forth all the glories of Him of whom this text speaks. . . . [I] will try to speak of men being blessed in Him. That is a note a little lower; if we cannot reach the highest octave, we may attain to a lower one; yet, while we speak of the blessing that comes from Him, let us still think of Him from whom the blessing comes, and let us remember that, as all blessings come from Him, it is because all blessings are laid up in Him; because every conceivable good is stored up in the person of the Lord Jesus Christ.[11]

The state of being blessed in God reflects several truths:
- We cannot abide in God's blessings unless we are connected to Him.
- That connection occurs when we accept Jesus Christ as our Redeemer.

- Being blessed in Him manifests when we can say without doubt, "I am God's child; the Father's love is set upon me. I have a part in the covenant of grace. I know without question that I am saved by the power of His blood." It is then and only then that we can abide in God's blessings.

The supernatural blessings that Christ gives to those who abide in Him were provided at the cross. He took our past in its entirety—with all its darkness, with all its sin—and paid the penalty due on our account. He made a clean sweep of our transgressions and declared to those who trust in Him, "Your sins are forgiven" (Luke 7:48).

Those who abide in God's blessings not only experience *past favor* through the redemptive blood of Jesus Christ but have the opportunity to walk in *present favor*. Every believer is blessed to be called a child of God and an heir of heaven. We are blessed to take our troubles to His throne of grace. We are blessed to have a Helper who will protect and deliver us from the snares of this world, for God's *present favor* surrounds us like a shield.

> *God's present favor surrounds us like a shield.*

We have all felt at one time or another as if we were walking on the tightrope of life. One misstep on our faith-walk and we fall into the depths of doubt and despair. However, abiding in God's blessing means that if we were to slip off the rope on which God calls us to walk, we are assured that underneath it are His everlasting arms, protecting us from the fall and cradling us in His mercy and grace.

Those who abide in God's blessings can also walk in *future favor*. He promises to see us through every trial and declares that nothing shall harm us—He will bring us safely to our journey's end, walking with us without fear through death's cold stream and causing us to rise victorious on the shore of the glistening city on the other side. Here we shall stand before His throne without a veil between us and our Redeemer, forever and for all eternity.[12]

Abiding in His blessings doesn't necessarily mean living in constant happiness. Compared with all that the word *blessed* implies, the word *happy* has no eternity, no depth, no fullness—no power—in it. I, for one, desire nothing more than to abide in God's blessings, surrounded by His favor, mercy, and grace. I want to savor every day as a gift of God. I hope to take nothing for granted, knowing that His blessings manifest in the subtlest of ways; for as I grow older, I realize more and more that I may never truly know the value of a moment until it becomes a cherished memory.

> *I may never truly know the value of a moment until it becomes a cherished memory.*

LIFE STORIES

There are no better examples of life stories that reflect the topic of abiding in God's blessings or living under the Enemy's curses than the lives of the people we have been reading about in 1 Samuel. Elkanah, Hannah, and Samuel were models of obedience, while Eli and his sons were models of disobedience.

> Then [Moses] took the Book of the Covenant and read in the hearing of the people. And they said, "All that the LORD has said we will do, and be obedient." (Exodus 24:7)

> Now it shall come to pass, if you diligently obey the voice of the LORD your God, to observe carefully all His commandments which I command you today, that the LORD your God will set you high above all nations of the earth. And all these blessings shall come upon you and overtake you, because you obey the voice of the LORD your God: "Blessed shall you be in the city, and blessed shall you be in the country." (Deuteronomy 28:1–3)

> But it shall come to pass, if you do not obey the voice of the LORD your God, to observe carefully all His commandments and His statutes which I command you today, that all these curses will come upon you and overtake you: "Cursed shall you be in the city, and cursed shall you be in the country." (Deuteronomy 28:15–16)

The Hebrew word for "obey" (*shema*) means "to hear or listen." This word exemplifies the difference between the Hebrew definition, which stresses physical action, and the Greek and Western mind-set, which emphasizes mental response.[13] Listening is a mental activity, and "hearing" in this context means that our ears pick up sounds. But in Hebrew, *shema* not only describes the mental act of hearing but the effects of *heeding* what we hear, such as being obedient and doing what is asked of us. Almost every place we see the word *obey* in the Bible, it derives from the root word *shema.*

Shema is also the traditional "pledge of allegiance" to God that observant Jews from biblical times to this day declare every morning and evening. It is the first word of the first line: "Hear [Shema], O Israel: The LORD our God, the LORD is one! You shall love the LORD your God with all your heart, with all your soul, and with all your strength" (Deuteronomy 6:4–5). By reciting this prayer, righteous Jews are reminded of their commitment to love the one true God of Abraham, Isaac, and Jacob; to dedicate themselves to following Him and Him alone; and to faithfully do His will.

The meaning of both the word and the prayer is to take heed, to listen and obey. It is the central affirmation of a Jewish person's commitment to the Lord. Many Jews teach the *Shema* to their children as soon as the children learn to talk because it is considered the most important prayer they can live by. So when Jesus said, "He who has ears to hear, let him hear!" (Matthew 11:15), He was calling believers to not merely listen to His words but to obey by putting them into action.

"Be doers of the Word, and not hearers only," instructs the writer in James 1:22. Some Christians put all the emphasis on what they think in their minds or hold in their hearts or say with their mouths, meanwhile considering physical action "dead works." However, the Hebrews understood that God's people cannot truly put what is heard in God's Word into their minds, hearts, and mouths until it transforms their lives as well, as demonstrated by their actions.

Everything we read about Hannah and her husband indicates that they heard God's Word and they heeded His voice. I'm confident that their obedience to God's mandates positively influenced the life of Samuel and the lives of the other children born to them.

There is an intense distinction between the character of Israel's corrupt worship represented by the disobedience of Eli's sons and the devout reverence and obedience of Samuel and his parents. Equally, there is a vivid contrast between the rewards and curses afforded these diverse families.

The Obedience of Elkanah and Hannah

They were obedient in:

- Worship and sacrifices (Read 1 Samuel 1:3, 7, 19, 21, 28; 2:19, 21.)
- Prayer (Read 1 Samuel 1:10; 2:1.)
- Their vows (Read 1 Samuel 1:11, 24, 27–28.)

The Obedience of Samuel

- Samuel ministered to the Lord. (Read 1 Samuel 2:11,18; 3:1.)
- He was obedient to delegated authority. (Read 1 Samuel 3:4–9.)
- He was obedient to God. (Read 1 Samuel 3:10.)

The Results of Obedience

- Samuel witnessed the blessing of the Lord upon his parents. (Read 1 Samuel 2:20–21.)

- He was chosen by the Lord. (Read 1 Samuel 2:21.)
- The boy "grew in stature, and in favor both with the LORD and men." (Read 1 Samuel 2:26.)
- Samuel was established and sustained as the Lord's prophet, evidenced by God's presence in him. (Read 1 Samuel 3:19–20.)
- Samuel became God's spokesman to the people. (Read 1 Samuel 3:21–4:1.)

The Disobedience of Eli

- This High Priest and father allowed his sons to disobey the Lord's commands concerning tabernacle sacrifices and offerings. (Read 1 Samuel 2:13–17, 29.)
- Eli put his sons and personal pride ahead of the Lord. (Read 1 Samuel 2:29.)
- Eli did not discipline his sons. (Read 1 Samuel 3:13.)

The Disobedience of Eli's Sons

- Hophni and Phinehas despised the Lord's sacrifices and offerings. (Read 1 Samuel 2:13–17.)
- Eli's sons disobeyed the Lord's moral commands. (Read 1 Samuel 2:22.)
- They did not obey their father. (Read 1 Samuel 2:25.)

The Results of Disobedience

- Eli's sons were corrupt; they did not know the Lord. (Read 1 Samuel 2:12.)
- Their disobedient example caused the Lord's people to sin. (Read 1 Samuel 2:17, 24.)

- The house of Eli was judged by God. (Read 1 Samuel 2:27–36; 3:11–14.)
- Hophni and Phinehas died on the same day, and they preceded their father in death. (Read 1 Samuel 2:34; 4:11.)
- The ark of the covenant was removed from Shiloh. This symbolized the devastating reality that God had removed His presence from Israel, a consequence that caused Eli's tragic death. (Read Samuel 4:3–5.)

Even though Phinehas and Hophni lacked the integrity that was essential to serve God, Eli allowed his two sons to continue to hold the office of priest. They not only stole from the sacrifices that were offered to God (1 Samuel 12:17), they also had sexual encounters with unescorted women who came to offer their sacrifices at the tabernacle of meeting (1 Samuel 2:22). The evil conduct of these two young men was a blatant affront to their sacred position, yet their father, the High Priest, "did not restrain them" (1 Samuel 3:13).

Eli had no power to change his sons' hearts, but he did have the authority to remove them from holy service, for they "abhorred the offering of the LORD" (1 Samuel 2:17). In spite of their openly rebellious and revolting behavior, Eli allowed them to defame the name of the Lord and lead the people of God astray.

The vile and corrupt conduct of Hophni and Phinehas, coupled with Eli's own passive parenting, brought a curse on their father's house (1 Samuel 2:27–36; 3:11–14), and as the Lord promised, both sons died in one day in the devastating battle with the Philistines at Aphek (1 Samuel 4:11). Eli wanted the approval of the sons he loved so very much, yet ironically, his weakness eventually led to their demise—and his.

Despite his shortcomings, Eli was still spiritually sensitive enough to acknowledge that he had brought the holy cause of the Lord of hosts into ridicule. It is significant to note that when Eli heard of his sons' deaths, he did not seem deeply grieved. It was as if he had previously mourned their spiritual death, so that now their physical death was almost a secondary consequence. However, when Eli learned that the enemy had captured the ark of the Lord, he was struck with unimaginable grief.

This very sad ending to Eli's life indicates that he truly loved God, and Scripture confirms it: "His heart trembled for the ark of God. . . . Then it happened, as he made mention of the ark of God, that Eli fell off the seat backward by the side of the gate; and his neck was broken and he died . . . " (1 Samuel 4:13, 18).

Eli's failure as a parent along with his sons' horrific conduct resulted in the boys' mutual death both morally and physically, as well as the continued spiritual collapse of Israel. Most importantly, Eli realized that in not administering the righteous discipline that his sons' conduct required, he had contributed to the exodus of God from Shiloh. In fulfillment of the Lord's prophecy against Eli's house, God saw to it that "you [Eli] will see an enemy in My dwelling place, despite all the good which God does for Israel" (1 Samuel 2:32).

At the wicked behavior of the people, God abandoned the tabernacle of Shiloh. For 340 years, the tribe of Ephraim had been blessed with the presence of the sacred ark, but now that honor was lost (Psalm 78:60, 67). Eventually the ark's safeguarding was transferred to the tribe of Judah at Mount Zion (Psalm 78:68; 87:2; 132:13), but the ark never returned to Shiloh. The light of its candlestick was taken away because the people had left their first love. Eventually their city dwindled to nothing. God's abandonment of Shiloh—and the people's mutual abandonment of God—was a warning according to the prophet Jeremiah: "But go now to My place which *was* in Shiloh, where I set My name at the first, and see what I did to it because of the wickedness of My people Israel" (Jeremiah 7:12).

I don't want to characterize Eli as a wicked man, for if he was, God would have destroyed him long before bringing Samuel to the tabernacle. Eli was a decent man who loved the Lord, but he apparently did not have the fortitude to fulfill the demanding role as Israel's High Priest. Eli had inherited a dysfunctional priesthood in Shiloh—he did not create it. However, he chose to perpetuate it, for there is no biblical indication that he did anything more than to passively man his position. His weaknesses allowed the problematic manmade traditions that operated in Shiloh—ones that opposed God's authorized rituals and worship protocols— to continue.[14]

The first line of chapter 3 of the book of 1 Samuel states the result: "The word of the LORD was rare in those days; there was no widespread revelation." There was no widespread prophetic revelation during these corrupt times because when God did speak, the people refused to listen.

Heaven's deafening silence is often a form of divine judgment. When the people turned their ear away from God, it resulted in Israel's downfall. But as always, God's mercy prevailed, for the calling of Samuel marked the end of God's silence.

Eli's faults as a father were reflected in the character of his sons. So why did the Almighty allow Eli to mentor Samuel? It was only because of God's grace and mercy. Were it not for Samuel's training in Shiloh's temple, Eli would have only been remembered as the High Priest whose derelict leadership caused the presence of

God to depart from Shiloh. Perhaps Eli's kind nature inclined the young Samuel to even more faithfully execute his temple duties. In any case, God enabled Eli to teach Samuel to listen for and obey the voice of God, even though Eli had not done this with his own sons.

The Loan

From the moment that I read, "Therefore I also have lent him to the LORD" (1 Samuel 1:28), I was determined to understand why this term was used. I stated previously that the word *loan* has several meanings, and another definition is "the permission to use something for a period of time." In our Western mentality, it means to give and then take back. However, Hannah would never revoke her vow, and she did not plan to call Samuel back to her, so why did she use the term?

Hannah used the Hebrew form of the word *Shaol*, which has as one of its meanings "the hollow of the hand." She was placing her child in God's care, for Samuel's name not only meant "Asked *of* God" but also "Lent or Given *to* God."

Let us review certain truths regarding what we give or present to God:

- Whatever we give to God is what we have first asked and received from Him (Matthew 7:8).
- All our gifts to God were first His gifts to us: "But who am I, and who are my people, that we should be able to offer so willingly as this? For all things come from You, and of Your own we have given You" (1 Chronicles 29:14).
- Whatever we give to God is placed in our heavenly bank, so to speak. He promises to repay it, with interest, to our immeasurable and indescribable benefit (Luke 6:38).

Hannah asked God for a son, and He gave her the desire of her heart. In fulfillment of her vow, Hannah placed Samuel in God's permanent care. Hannah's sacrifice was indeed great—it could not have been made without God's divine grace and strength. Yet the more we give to God, the more He gives back to us. And He adds an abundance of spiritual blessings as well.

> *Whatever we give to God is placed*
> *in our heavenly bank, so to speak.*
> *He promises to repay it,*
> *with interest, to our immeasurable*
> *and indescribable benefit.*

Hannah had lovingly nurtured Samuel while he lived with her in Ramah. She taught him to give praise to the Lord, who is the source of every good gift. The Talmud teaches that denying a child religious knowledge robs the child of an inheritance.[15] Hannah made sure Samuel was taught well, for the Talmud also says, "Who is best taught? He that is taught of his mother."[16]

I have often thought of Hannah leaving her young son in Shiloh, knowing that she would see him only a few times a year. Somehow the Lord of hosts had given this first-time mother the assurance that no matter how she and her son might be separated in this world, everything was going to be all right.

We know that, according to the divinely mandated schedule of Jewish festivals, Hannah would see Samuel at least three times a year when Elkanah took his family to Shiloh, but in my study, I questioned whether Samuel ever visited Hannah in Ramah. And what I expected was confirmed:

- Samuel was born and dedicated in Ramah: "Then they rose early in the morning and worshiped before the LORD, and returned and came to their house at Ramah. And Elkanah knew Hannah his wife, and the LORD remembered her. So it came to pass in the process of time that Hannah conceived and bore a son, and called his name Samuel, saying, 'Because I have asked for him from the LORD'" (1 Samuel 1:19–20).

- Samuel judged Israel from Ramah: "But he always returned to Ramah, for his home was there. There he judged Israel, and there he built an altar to the LORD" (1 Samuel 7:17).

- Samuel called for spiritual meetings in Ramah: "Then all the elders of Israel gathered together and came to Samuel at Ramah" (1 Samuel 8:4).

- Samuel returned to Ramah after he painfully separated himself from King Saul: "Then Samuel went to Ramah, and Saul went up to his house at Gibeah of Saul" (1 Samuel 15:34).

- Samuel went to Ramah after anointing King David: "Then Samuel took the horn of oil and anointed him in the midst of his brothers; and the Spirit of the LORD came upon David from that day forward. So Samuel arose and went to Ramah" (1 Samuel 16:13).

- David found Samuel in Ramah when he fled Saul: "So David fled and escaped, and went to Samuel at Ramah, and told him all that Saul had done to him. And he and Samuel went and stayed in Naioth" (1 Samuel 19:18).

- Samuel established his School of Prophets in Ramah: "Now it was told Saul, saying, 'Take note, David is at Naioth in Ramah!' Then Saul sent messengers to take David. And when they saw the group of prophets prophesying, and Samuel standing as leader over them, the Spirit of God came upon the messengers of Saul, and they also prophesied" (1 Samuel 19:19–20).

- Samuel died at his home in Ramah: "Then Samuel died; and the Israelites gathered together and lamented for him, and buried him at his home in Ramah. And David arose and went down to the Wilderness of Paran" (1 Samuel 25:1).

Samuel called Ramah his home, and he honored his mother and father every opportunity he had with his presence and through his actions. His private existence exemplified his public teachings, and even though Samuel was not a Nazarite, he embodied a simple, self-denying, and unpretentious life. Samuel was kind to the poor; he was hospitable to friends and always available to serve the Lord every day, in every way, and for all of his life (1 Samuel 7:34, 3:10, 12:2).

Hannah never would have predicted that Samuel would be with her in Ramah as often as he was. This woman of faith selflessly submitted her child to the Lord, and He, in turn, honored Hannah's faithful sacrifice by fulfilling her vow in Samuel's life and allowing mother and son to be regularly reunited.

Hannah's powerful connection with the Lord enriched her life with God's blessing and favor.

SPIRITUAL CHECKLIST

1. Elkanah favored Hannah over Peninnah and surrounded her
    with special kindness and attention, yet Hannah could never
    fully benefit from those blessings because she was so con-
    sumed with her desire for a child. Do you find yourself doing
    as Hannah did? *List those blessings—those moments in time
    where you have not fully appreciated the favor of God because you
    were so consumed by a trial or because you were waiting on an
    answer to your prayer.*

    _____

    _____

    _____

    _____

    _____

    _____

    _____

    _____

    _____

2. Based on Torah mandate, Hannah and Elkanah blessed their
    children at every opportunity. *Do you proclaim blessings over
    your loved ones? If you are a mother, list the names of your chil-
    dren and the blessings that you desire for their lives. If you are*

not a mother, list the names of your loved ones along with a corresponding blessing. Once you have written the blessings down, begin to declare them over your family every day.

3. Eli did not discipline his sons, and consequently, he and his sons suffered severe judgment. *Do you as a parent lovingly discipline your children? Do you teach them the statutes of God? Do you set forth a godly example for their lives? Closely evaluate your answers to the above questions and list the ways you can improve.*

STEP OF FAITH

Every believer has the opportunity to walk in God's favor. The effects of our communion with the Lord should be the joy we experience in His unwavering character, His faithful promises, and His gracious answers to prayer.

Write down your personal step of faith that will enable you to better abide in God's blessings.

> *For You, O LORD, will bless the righteous;*
> *with favor You will surround him as with a shield.*
>
> PSALM 5:12

PROCLAMATION

In the name of Jesus Christ of Nazareth, I am the righteousness of God; therefore, I am entitled to covenant blessings and favor. The favor of God is among the righteous. His favor surrounds the righteous; therefore, it surrounds me. Everywhere I go, in everything I do, I expect the favor of God to be manifested. Never again will I be without the favor of God.

Satan, my days of lack and want cease today. I am going from the pit to the palace because the favor of God is upon me. It rests richly on me. It profusely abounds in me, and I am part of the generation that will experience the favor of God in immeasurable and limitless ways.

Therefore, God's favor produces in my life supernatural increase and promotion, good health and abundant joy, prominence, restoration and honor, preferential treatment and increased assets, great victories, petitions granted, policies and rules changed on my behalf, and battles won that I don't have to fight.

The favor of God is upon me—it walks behind me to protect me from evil, it walks beside me to be my constant companion, and it goes before me to guide my perfect path. From this day forward, I will abide in God's blessings, and my life will never be the same. Amen.

Chapter 9

Significance— Destined for Greatness

❦

*You shall increase my greatness,
and comfort me on every side.*

PSALM 71:21

SCRIPTURAL FOUNDATIONS

Read 1 Samuel 3:1–4, 10, 19–21; 10:1; 16:13.

Verses 3:1–4: *Now the boy Samuel ministered to the LORD before Eli. And the word of the LORD was rare in those days; there was no widespread revelation. And it came to pass at that time, while Eli was lying down in his place, and when his eyes had begun to grow so dim that he could not see, and before the lamp of God went out in the tabernacle of the* LORD *where the ark of God was, and while Samuel was lying down, that the* LORD *called Samuel. And he answered, "Here I am!"*

These verses set the stage for the imminent ascendancy of Samuel to the position of Israel's judge and prophet. As Eli was growing weaker, the Lord prepared to place the mantle of leadership on his protégé. The young Samuel did not yet recognize the voice of the Great I AM (1 Samuel 3:5–9), nor did he realize that he would be chosen to receive the "glow of the still burning lamp of *Hashem* [Hebrew for 'The Name']."[1] But Eli knew who was calling the boy, and he guided Samuel in how to respond.

Verse 3:10: *Now the* LORD *came and stood and called as at other times, "Samuel! Samuel!" And Samuel answered, "Speak, for Your servant hears."*

God called Samuel again, and at Eli's instruction, the young man humbly uttered the words that would sculpt his future relationship with the Lord.

Verses 3:19–21: *So Samuel grew, and the* LORD *was with him and let none of his words fall to the ground. And all Israel from Dan to Beersheba knew that Samuel had been established as a prophet of the* LORD. *Then the* LORD *appeared again in Shiloh. For the* LORD *revealed Himself to Samuel in Shiloh by the word of the* LORD.

These verses announce the drastic disparity between Samuel's era of prophetic leadership and the declining years of Eli. The prophetic voice of the Lord within Israel had greatly diminished due to the disgraceful conduct of the people, spearheaded by Eli's sons. As a result, both Eli and the city of Shiloh lost their prominence among their countrymen. Jewish scholars believe that God's presence would have entirely departed from Shiloh had it not been for Samuel's virtue.

> *Jewish scholars believe that God's presence would have entirely departed from Shiloh had it not been for Samuel's virtue.*

This young man exemplified a reverence for God and integrity before the people; therefore, the Lord honored everything he said. This trust cultivated a national confidence in Samuel and produced a desire within Israel to turn back to God. Because of Samuel's righteous leadership, the Lord restored His presence to an even greater degree than before, and prophecy again became widespread throughout the land.[2] The spiritual drought in Israel was over.

Verse 10:1 *Then Samuel took a flask of oil and poured it on [Saul's] head, and kissed him and said: "Is it not because the LORD has anointed you commander over His inheritance?"*

Verse 16:13: *Then Samuel took the horn of oil and anointed [David] in the midst of his brothers; and the Spirit of the LORD came upon David from that day forward. So Samuel arose and went to Ramah.*

Samuel was chosen by the Lord to anoint Israel's first two kings, Saul and David. It is interesting to note that God's prophet anointed Saul with a *flask* of oil while he anointed David with a *horn* of oil. What was the difference?

Samuel anointed Saul with a fragile earthen vessel made by human hands, symbolic of the temporary nature of his kingship (forty years [Acts 13:21]), whereas he used a God-created vessel to anoint David, signifying the permanency of his kingdom (2 Kings 9:5; Isaiah 9:7). Scholars note that there was also a difference in the oil used to anoint both kings. God commanded Moses to create a compound of oil and spices with which to anoint and consecrate the tabernacle, its vessels, and the priests (Exodus 30:22– 32). This exclusive oil was reported to have remained intact and undiminished despite its perpetual use in anointing every High Priest and king in the Davidic dynasty until the reign of King Josiah.

When the destruction of Solomon's temple became imminent, this holy oil and the ark were hidden, and they will remain concealed until the coming of the Messiah. Since Saul was not in the Davidic line, Samuel used a different mixture of oil (*balsamum*) to anoint him, and he used the consecrated oil to anoint David as king.[3]

LIFE APPLICATION

Whom will he teach knowledge? And whom will he make
to understand the message? Those just weaned from milk?
Those just drawn from the breasts?
ISAIAH 28:9

Hannah had dedicated her beloved Samuel to the Lord of hosts before his birth, and later she lent him to His service in fulfillment of that vow. Hannah and Elkanah were righteous believers in the Great I AM and doers of His Word. I am confident that while Hannah was weaning Samuel, Elkanah laid hands on and declared blessings over their son every Sabbath. While Hannah physically nurtured Samuel with mother's milk, she also spiritually nurtured him with her daily song of praise to God.

I can hear Hannah's voice daily declaring God's favor over her precious child as that momentous journey to Shiloh approached. Once there, Hannah repeated her vow; she was announcing to God in His tabernacle that no matter how much she loved her miracle baby, she was still willing to keep her promise to Him.

In honor of Hannah's vow and Samuel's loyal and devoted service, God made her son one of the most esteemed men in all of Scripture. Samuel's accomplishments would be Hannah's accomplishments and his legacy her legacy. Samuel was destined for greatness.

> *Samuel's accomplishments*
> *would be Hannah's accomplishments*
> *and his legacy her legacy.*

Samuel's Legacy

Even though the presence of God had diminished in Shiloh, He was not absent. In every age God surrounds His people with His presence. In every age He is infinitely near. In every age He stands at the door and knocks. And in every age God's people fail to recognize Him. Therefore, when we face difficulties, God may seem distant or even nonexistent to us, but He is never absent.

It had been three hundred years since the death of Moses, and though God had addressed Israel through a few "foothill" individuals, there had been no "mountain-top" personalities to equal Moses. Throughout his life, this great prophet kept the sense of God before the people. When Moses left, it was as if God had left, because all they had seen of Him was through the character of Moses.[4] But now God was back!

Samuel inherited a faith implanted by his mother and father and further taught to him by Eli, but when he heard directly from God, his faith was now born out of personal experience. Samuel, like Moses, became a man who knew God so intimately that he was able to be a revelation of the Lord to others. When the people of Israel saw Samuel, they witnessed the Spirit of God in him.

The following are but a few of Samuel's accomplishments.

Judge

"Samuel judged Israel all the days of his life" (1 Samuel 7:15).

This verse records the fulfillment of Hannah's vow (1 Samuel 1:11, 28); however, the whole of chapter 7 establishes Samuel as judge, prophet, and leader over the nation of Israel. Jewish scholars consider him equal to Moses and Aaron combined. Samuel assumed this distinguished leadership position at the age of thirty-nine and held it for eleven years, until the reign of King Saul began.

The office of judge was similar to that of king, for it carried with it great power. Samuel visited the people of Israel, heard their grievances, and helped settle their disputes (1 Samuel 7:16–17). He maintained the law and authority of God, rebuked iniquity, and restrained and sentenced transgressors in high places (such as King Saul). Samuel challenged Israel's national immorality and insisted that Israel separate itself from the heathen nations and their customs.[5]

During his tenure, Samuel traveled the entire country to judge, teach, and reprove God's people. He also led a spiritual and historical revolution by calling the nation of Israel to mass repentance and by ending the Philistine domination, leading Israel into victory against its enemy in Mizpah (1 Samuel 7:7–12).

Prophet

"After that He gave them judges for about four hundred and fifty years, until Samuel the prophet" (Acts 13:20).

A prophet is one who is in close communion with God. So close that the Lord allows him or her to pull back the curtain from the secret counsels of heaven to reveal His hidden truths and foreshadow coming events. Hannah's Levite son was such a man; he became the moral compass for the people of Israel.

With Samuel, Israel's history came alive with prophetic revelation. He set forth such a great example of the office that he became known as the father of all great prophets.[6]

Leader and Teacher

"Then Saul sent messengers to take David. And when they saw the group of prophets prophesying, and Samuel standing as leader over them, the Spirit of God came upon the messengers of Saul, and they also prophesied" (1 Samuel 19:20).

Samuel was the high point of the era of the judges. The nation of Israel, from the time of Moses until the anointing of King Saul, had been a theocracy—a system of government in which priests, judges, or prophets ruled in the name of God. Samuel was the end of this theocracy and the implementer of a monarchy.

Samuel would become the trusted confidant to kings—a leader of leaders. When Saul in his spirit of rebellion sinned against God, he confessed to Samuel (1 Samuel 15: 24). And when David found himself in a time of trouble, he went straight to Ramah because he knew God's prophet would provide him with wisdom in his time of distress. Samuel had given David God's assurance of the crown, and since David's faith in that assurance was beginning to fail, he needed Samuel's sound encouragement (1 Samuel 19:18).

Samuel also founded the first School of Prophets and located it in Naoith, a suburb of Ramah, his birthplace (1 Samuel 19:18–19, 22).

The "band of prophets" referred to in 1 Samuel 19 was most likely a group of Levitical students of Samuel's who served in tabernacle roles and ceremonial worship. These men are mentioned in connection with Ramah (1 Samuel 19:18), Beth-el (2 Kings 2:3), Jericho (2 Kings 2:5), and Gilgal (2 Kings 4:38)—all places central to the career of Samuel. This is why historians believe that it was Samuel who established each school.[7]

The schools served as barriers against widespread corruption by providing moral and spiritual guidance to those who were qualified to act in the fear of God. These students became leaders and counselors to the people of God, and their purpose was to ensure Israel's future by establishing and upholding its moral and physical prosperity.[8]

Moses and Aaron were among His priests,
and Samuel was among those who called
upon His name; they called upon the LORD,
and He answered them.

PSALM 99:6

The heartbeat of Samuel's entire life was his faithful love for and reverent dedication to the Lord of hosts. He grew up in daily contact with the holy things of God. He learned the sacred rituals, names, and symbols that the Lord had given to Moses and to the lineage of priests that followed. Samuel knew from an early age that he had been set apart by his mother for the service of the Lord. And in fulfillment of Hannah's vow, Samuel reverently and humbly served the Lord who called him by name (1 Samuel 3).

LIFE STORIES

When human history has been at a crossroads, God has often used a woman whose life and actions changed the destiny of the world. Susanna Wesley was such a woman.

Susanna

Susanna Annesley was born in 1669. She married Samuel Wesley, an Anglican minister, in 1689. She bore nineteen children and served the Lord until her death at the age of seventy-three. As a wife and mother in a small eighteenth-century English parish, Susanna Wesley received little recognition for how she managed her household, raising and educating so many children and coping with a sometimes debt-ridden, unrealistic, and often-challenging husband.

Susanna and Samuel lived in constant strife. Twice their homes were burned to the ground and they lost everything they owned. Because of her husband's gross mismanagement of their finances and negligence of responsibility, Susanna was often plagued by debt and left alone with her children for long periods of time.

Nine of their children died in infancy, and two of the ten who lived were physically impaired. Yet despite these challenges and her own lifelong bouts with illness, Susanna managed to care for her cherished children, teach them social skills, and educate them— but more importantly, instill in them the unconditional love of God.

Susanna, who knew Greek, Latin, and French, painstakingly taught her ten children for six hours each day. Among her practical lessons was to say the Lord's Prayer every morning and evening, sing hymns three times a day, and walk in faith without apology. A quote that best describes her practical application of the gospel is: "Whatever weakens your reason, impairs the tenderness of your conscience, obscures your sense of God, takes off your relish for spiritual things, whatever increases the authority of the body over the mind, that thing is sin to you, however innocent it may seem in itself."

Susanna taught her children a very simple lesson about their faith: "Believe it and behave it." She stated, "The child that never learns to obey his parents in the home will not obey God or man out of the home." This dedicated mother trained her older children to instruct the younger in Bible study and prayers before breakfast and after dinner. One scholar described the Wesley children as "a cluster of bright, vehement, argumentative boys and girls, living by a clean and high code, and on the plainest fare; but drilled to soft tones, to pretty formal courtesies; with learning as an ideal, duty as an atmosphere and fear of God as law."[9]

The well-disciplined Susanna made it a rule to spend an hour a day with each child over the period of a week, giving them personal time to discuss "principal concerns" and also allowing her to provide spiritual direction. After their home burned down in 1709, she paid special attention to John, who was almost lost in the fire. She vowed to the Lord, "[I] intended to be more particularly careful of the soul of this child that Thou hast so mercifully provided for, than ever I have been, that I may do my endeavors to instill into his mind the disciplines of Thy true religion and virtue."[10]

As a young woman, Susanna promised to devote two hours of daily prayer to the Lord. She did not recognize then that in later life she would be left alone to manage and care for her entire household. Struggling to find a time and place to set herself apart to be with God within her hectic day, she finally informed her children that when they saw her apron over her head, it meant she was in prayer and shouldn't be disturbed.[11]

No matter how hard life became or how desperate her situation, she was always devoted to her walk with Christ, to praying for her children, and to instilling in them the knowledge of His Word. On one occasion, Susanna's son John wrote his mother and asked her to give him advice on how to raise children. Susanna replied with an in-depth letter detailing her child-rearing philosophies. Among them were:

- Teach a child to pray as soon as he can speak.
- To prevent lying, punish no fault that is first confessed and repented of.
- Any attempt to please, even if poorly performed, should be commended.
- Never punish a child twice for a single offense.

John Wesley later said of his mother, "I learned more about Christianity from my mother than from all the theologians in England."

While Samuel was on one of his extended stays in London, he assigned an interim minister to preach in his absence. Susanna believed this preacher was inadequately serving her children's spiritual needs, so since there were no church services on Sunday evenings, she organized a family gathering in her home where she and the children sang psalms and prayed, and Susanna read a short sermon from her husband's library. Word spread of Susanna's "Kitchen Meeting," and neighbors began to attend. Soon the prayer meeting became so popular that as many as three hundred people gathered.

The interim minister considered her meeting direct competition and asked Samuel to order Susanna to discontinue it. Believing in the conviction of her heart that the assembly was good and effective, Susanna respectfully responded to her husband's letter with these words:

> If you do, after all, think fit to dissolve this assembly, do not tell me that you desire me to do it, for that will not satisfy my conscience: but send me your positive command, in such full and express terms as may absolve me from all guilt and punishment for neglecting this opportunity of doing good when you and I shall appear before the great and awful tribunal of our Lord Jesus Christ.[12]

The services continued.

Setting her personal ambitions aside, Susanna used her influence to foster a spiritual awakening in her children that would fill a void in the religious life of a nation. She once wrote, "I look upon every soul under my charge as a talent committed to me under a trust. I am not a man nor a minister, but I spare every night to discourse with each child apart, strengthening their tiny faith in God our Savior."

The Methodist movement would eventually become a worldwide church due to the foundations of faith established in the home by a righteous woman. This is a great legacy from one who expressed this simple desire: "I am content to fill a little space if God be glorified."

Susanna's Son John

John Wesley became an Anglican minister and theologian who, along with his brother Charles and evangelist George Whitefield, is credited with founding the evangelical movement known as Methodism. His extensive preaching and wide-ranging writings also played a leading role in the development of the Holiness movement and Pentecostalism.[16] John Wesley rode over 250,000 miles on horseback and preached over 40,000 sermons (sometimes three a day) to hundreds of thousands of people in his lifetime.[13]

Of his salvation experience, John wrote, "I felt I did trust in Christ, Christ alone for salvation; and an assurance was given me that He had taken away my sins, even mine, and saved me from the law of sin and death." He was able to translate his knowledge and experiences into more than five thousand published sermons, tracts, and pamphlets designed for the common man. Because of his enormous output, John Wesley is also considered "The Father of the Religious Paperback."[14]

In addition, John was an avid abolitionist who, along with his friends John Newton and William Wilberforce, stood against slave trade. In 1774, he published a pamphlet on slavery entitled *Thoughts Upon Slavery*, saying, "Liberty is the right of every human creature, as soon as he breathes the vital air; and no human law can deprive him of that right which he derives from the law of nature."

Because of his organizational genius—a trait he surely inherited from his mother—we know exactly how many followers John

Wesley had when he died: 294 preachers overseeing 71,668 British church members, nineteen missionaries (five in mission stations), and 43,265 American church members with 198 preachers. Today, Methodists number about thirty million worldwide.

Susanna's Son Charles

John's younger brother Charles made an equally remarkable contribution to Christianity by writing nearly nine thousand hymns, including some of the most memorable songs of the church: "Hark! The Herald Angels Sing," "And Can It Be," "O for a Thousand Tongues to Sing," "Love Divine, All Loves Excelling," "Jesus, Lover of My Soul," "Christ the Lord Is Risen Today," "Soldiers of Christ, Arise," and "Rejoice! The Lord Is King!"

When the Anglican Church refused the brothers access to their pulpits due to their Methodist style of teaching, John and Charles began to preach in open-air meetings at the advice of evangelist Whitefield. During the five years encompassing 1739–1743, Charles computed in his journals that he preached to 149,400 people. Throughout his adult life, Charles produced fifty-six volumes of songs for use in Methodist meetings, with lyrics that his brother John described as containing a "distinct and full account of scriptural Christianity."

❧

Susanna Wesley not only influenced her family but also future generations of believers. She encouraged parishioners to communicate their faith in a manner that could be understood by family members, friends, and society. Her writings challenged women to become defenders of the faith, articulate teachers, and effective evangelists of "practical divinity," first to our children and then to the world. And as death drew near, she approached this as she approached everything else in her life: with Christian assurance and triumph.

Her son John noted in one of his writings that as her soul was freed of the weight of this life, "we stood around the bed and fulfilled her last request, uttered a little before she lost her speech, 'Children, as soon as I am released, sing a psalm of praise to God.'"[15] Susanna's children honored her in life, and they obeyed her in death—gathering around her bedside and singing a song of triumph. Of the many lessons this woman of valor taught them, certainly among the most important was to strive for a new intimacy with God.

Susanna Wesley never personally preached a sermon, published a book, or founded a church, yet her influence led two of her sons, John and Charles, to help launch a spiritual movement that crossed the Atlantic and awakened two nations on two different continents. From England to the shores of the fledgling American colonies, Susanna's place in Christian history is forever anchored in the accomplishments of her two sons. And it all began in her home, where she supplied John and Charles Wesley with the focused leadership that would both empower and inspire them to profoundly change history for the glory of the Lord. Susanna's sacrificial life birthed in them a movement that would bring the light of the gospel to a dark world for generations to come.

Susanna believed that all her children were destined for greatness. And *that's* what love looks like.

SPIRITUAL CHECKLIST

1. While the people of Samuel's time were destroyed by their own selfishness, Samuel stood out as a man of honor and integrity. As in his day, our society is in social and spiritual decay. Samuel chose to be the moral compass for Israel during this dark time. *Do others see God in you like they did in Samuel? If not, list the obstacles that keep you from reflecting the Lord in all that you do and say. If the answer is yes, then list those traits in you that best display God's presence in your life.*

2. Hannah prayed prayers of blessing over Samuel and instilled in him the desire to serve God. In spite of difficult circumstances, Susanna Wesley persevered and taught her children

the fundamentals of God's Word. *From their lives, list seven examples of the lessons we as women of God should teach our children.*

_____

_____

_____

_____

_____

_____

3. Susanna Wesley's prayer closet was her apron. Our loved ones should know that we are praying diligently for them no matter how busy we are or how hard the circumstances. *Where's your apron? Determine how you can create some space for prayer in the busyness of your life. Then list the names of your loved ones and what you are calling forth in their lives.*

_____

_____

_____

_____

_____

STEP OF FAITH

Samuel's willingness to serve God was the source of his strength. He exemplified the mind, disposition, and character of a faithful servant.

Are you prepared to serve the Lord when He calls? What step of faith can you take that testifies of your readiness to serve Him?

....

....

....

....

....

....

PROCLAMATION

Father—God of Abraham, Isaac, and Jacob—I praise You for Your infinite mercy and grace. I confess anything that I have done or said that has prevented those I influence to miss their divine destiny.

I thank You that You are a God of second chances, and I ask that You show me how I can instill in my biological and spiritual children Your eternal, unconditional love.

I declare that from this day forward, I will speak only words of blessing and encouragement over them, and that I will be an example that they can follow as I help prepare them to become vessels of greatness in Your Kingdom. Amen.

Chapter 10

The New Song

*Oh, sing to the L*ORD *a new song! Sing to the L*ORD,
*all the earth. Sing to the L*ORD, *bless His name; proclaim
the good news of His salvation [redemption] from day to day.
Declare His glory among the nations,
His wonders among all peoples.*

PSALM 96:1–3

The redemption of every believer occurs in three tenses: past, present, and future. The past tense took place when God delivered us from the guilt of sin through the death of Christ. We received this redemption the moment we confessed our sins and accepted Christ as Savior. This form of redemption is called *justification*.[1] (Read John 5:24; Romans 5:18.)

Hannah referred to the second—the present tense of God's redemption—in her prayer to the Lord (1 Samuel 2:1). It occurs when God saves us from the daily temptation and power of sin over the thoughts of our mind, the weakness of our flesh, and the acts of our will. This redemptive deliverance is called *sanctification*.[2] (Read 1 Corinthians 10:12–13; 2 Thessalonians 2:13–14.)

The final form of redemption happens in the future tense and occurs at the time of the believer's death. It is not deliverance from physical death but from spiritual death. This ultimate redemption is referred to as *glorification*.[3] (Read 1 John 3:2.)

We all stand at the threshold of the ultimate form of redemption. As in times past, it is the righteous woman whose song is the most poignant, whose tambourine is the most hopeful, whose dance is the most joyous. Our yearning for the Messiah's return runs deep. It inspires and uplifts, and it forms the dominant strain in the melody of redemption.[4]

The Midrash describes ten songs of unconditional praise (*Shira*) in the history of Israel. All were examples of the soul's spontaneous expressions of a deep yearning for and profound thankfulness to the Lord. The first was sung on the night of the exodus in Egypt (Isaiah 30:29). The second is the Song of Moses and Miriam at the Red Sea (Exodus 15:1–21). Next is the "Song at the Well," where the Lord provided water to the Israelites (Numbers 21:17–20). The fourth is the Song of Moses at the end of his life (Deuteronomy 31–32). The fifth was sung when God stopped the sun for Joshua (Joshua 10:12–13). Then there was the Song of Deborah in Judges 5, and King David's song of praise after his deliverance from his enemies (2 Samuel 22). The eighth was sung during the dedication of the Holy Temple (Psalm 30), and the ninth example was King Solomon's "Song of Songs" (Song of Solomon chapters 1-17).

The tenth song according to Jewish teaching will be the *shir chadash*, or "the New Song." It will be a song of the ultimate redemption of mankind: "A redemption that is global and absolute; a redemption that will annihilate all suffering, ignorance, jealousy, and hate from the face of the earth. This will be a redemption of such proportions that the yearning it evokes, and the joy it brings, requires a new song—a completely new musical vocabulary—to capture the voice of Creation's ultimate striving."[5]

> *As in times past, it is the righteous woman*
> *whose song is the most poignant,*
> *whose tambourine is the most hopeful,*
> *whose dance is the most joyous.*

All ten songs spring forth from a supernatural redemption. They are the outcome of an insightful appreciation of what could have happened had God not intervened. They are a result of a deep longing to be nearer to our Redeemer. And ultimately, each song glorifies the Creator.

One day soon we will stand with Hannah and others who have been saved by God's mercy and grace, and together we will sing the new song of the redeemed:

You [Lord of hosts] are worthy to take the scroll, and to open its seals; for You were slain, and have redeemed us to God by Your blood out of every tribe and tongue and people and nation, and have made us kings and priests to our God; and we shall reign on the earth. . . . Worthy is the Lamb who was slain to receive power and riches and wisdom, and strength and honor and glory and blessing! . . . Blessing and honor and glory and power be to Him who sits on the throne, and to the Lamb, forever and ever! (Revelation 5:9–10, 12–13)

Redemption is of the Lord, and it is by His grace that we are justified, sanctified, and glorified. God found nothing in us to merit our redemption; instead, He found it within Himself—then He freely gave it. And that, my dear friends, is what love truly looks like!

"I pray that out of his glorious riches he may
strengthen you with power through his Spirit
in your inner being, so that Christ
may dwell in your hearts through faith.
And I pray that you, being rooted and established in love,
may have power, together with all the Lord's holy people,
to grasp how wide and long and high
and deep is the love of Christ."
EPHESIANS 3:16–18 NIV

NOTES

Chapter 1

1. Diana Hagee, *Ruth: The Romance of Redemption* (Nashville, TN: Thomas Nelson, 2005), ix.
2. Derek Prince, *Foundational Truths for Christian Living* (Lake Mary, FL: Strang, 1993), 17–21.

Chapter 2

1. Spiros Zodhiates, ThD, ed., *Hebrew-Greek Key Word Study Bible*, 2nd rev. ed. (Chattanooga, TN: AMG, 2008), 373.
2. *The Hebrew Bible*, "The Eight Books of the Prophets (*Neviim*)" (Minneapolis, MN: Fortress Press, 2004).
3. *The Woman's Study Bible* (Nashville, TN: Thomas Nelson, 2013), 442.
4. J. Vernon McGee, *Through the Bible*, vol. 2 (Nashville, TN: Thomas Nelson, 1994), 123.
5. Matthew George Easton, ed., *Easton's Bible Dictionary* (London: T. Nelson & Sons, 1897).
6. "Ancient Jewish History: The Ark of the Covenant," *Jewish Virtual Library*, http://www.jewishvirtuallibrary.org/jsource/Judaism/ark.html.
7. H. D. Spence, ed., *Samuel, The Pulpit Commentary 9*, vol. 1 (London and New York: Funk and Wagnalls, 1890), 1.
8. Ibid.
9. Finis Jennings Dake, ed., *Dake's Annotated Reference Bible* (Lawrenceville, GA: Dake Publishing, 2014), 500.
10. Ibid.
11. Nissan Mindel, "Eli-The High Priest," *Kehot Publication Society*, last modified July 2011, http://www.chabad.org/library/article_cdo/aid/112391/jewish/Eli-The-High-Priest.htm.
12. Ibid.
13. F.C. Cook, ed., "The First Book of Samuel," *The Bible Commentary: Exodus to Esther Barnes' Notes* (Grand Rapids: Baker Book House, 1983), 8.
14. Emil G. Hirsch, Wilhelm Bacher, and Jacob Zallel Lauterbach, eds., "Samuel," *Jewish Encyclopedia* (London and New York: Funk & Wagnall, 1901–1906), 106.
15. Ibid., 6.

Chapter 3
1. Ibid., Chapter 2, "Alphabetical Exposition of Named Bible Women."
2. The terms *sanctified*, *sorrow*, *supplication*, *song*, and *sacrifice* in reference to Hannah's story are taken from Herbert Lockyer, *All the Women of the Bible: Hannah, The Woman Who Personifies Ideal Motherhood* (Grand Rapids, MI: Zondervan, 1988).
3. John Hagee, ed., *The Prophecy Bible* (Nashville, TN: Thomas Nelson, 1997), 786–87.
4. Jim Gwinn, *A Life Well Lived: 52 Inspiring Real-life Stories for Devotion, Study and Family Reading* (Seattle, WA: CRISTA Ministries, 2005), 171–76.

Chapter 4
1. Tamar Kadari, "Hannah: Midrash and Aggadah," *Jewish Women: A Comprehensive Historical Encyclopedia*, Jewish Women's Archive, last modified March 20, 2009, http://jwa.org/encyclopedia/article/hannah -midrash-and-aggadah.
2. Ibid.
3. Ibid.
4. Rivkah Slonim, "The Mikvah," *Chabad.org*, 2004, http://www.chabad.org /theJewishWoman/article_cdo/aid/1541/jewish/The-Mikvah.htm.
5. Inspired by a story written by Alexander Woolcott, *Illustrations Unlimited* (Carrol Stream, IL: Tyndall House, 1988), 265–66.

Chapter 5
1. Tamar Kadari, "Hannah: Midrash and Aggadah," *Jewish Women: A Comprehensive Historical Encyclopedia*, Jewish Women's Archive, last modified March 20, 2009, http://jwa.org/encyclopedia/article/hannah -midrash-and-aggadah.
2. Nosson Scherman, *The Rubin Edition of the Prophets: Samuel 1 and 2*, Art Scroll series (New York: Mesorah Publications, 2002), 7.
3. A. W. Tozer, *The Knowledge of the Holy* (New York: HarperOne, 2009), 43.
4. Content in this section adapted from John McMillan, *The Authority of the Believer* (Camp Hill, PA: Wingspread Publishers, 2007), 25.
5. Olive Wyon, *The School of Prayer* (Whitefish, MT: Kessinger Publishing, 2010).

Chapter 6
1. Rabbi Louis Jacobs, "The Brit Milah (Bris) Ceremony," *My Jewish Learning*, http://www.myjewishlearning.com/article/the-brit-milah-bris-ceremony/2/#.
2. Cyrus Adler, S. Roubin, "Birthday," *Jewish Encyclopedia*, http://www .jewishencyclopedia.com/articles/3322-birthday.
3. Adapted from Clovis G. Chappell, *And the Prophets* (New York: Abingdon-Cokesbury Press, 1946), 9–19.

4. James Smith, *Handfuls on Purpose*, vol. I (Grand Rapids, MI: Wm. B. Eerdmans Publishing Company, 1943), 227.

5. Matthew Henry, *1 Peter, Matthew Henry Commentary on the Whole Bible (Complete)*, 1706, http://www.biblestudytools.com/commentaries/matthew-henry-complete/genesis/.

6. Adapted from Robert Lee, *Handfuls on Purpose*, vol. XI (Grand Rapids, MI: Wm. B. Eerdmans Publishing Company, 1943), 42.

7. Yad Vashem, "The Righteous Among the Nations," *The World Holocaust Remembrance Center*, http://www.yadvashem.org/yv/en/righteous/about.asp.

8. Yad Vashem, "Woman of Valor; Stories of Women who Rescued Jews During the Holocaust," "Irena Sendler," *The World Holocaust Remembrance Center*, http://www.yadvashem.org/yv/en/exhibitions/righteous-women/sendler.asp.

9. *The Jerusalem Talmud*, Sanhedrin 4:1 (22a) (London: Williams and Norgate, 1886).

10. A. Netanel, "Lulek: Child of Buchenwald," *Holocaust Studies*, 2006, http://www.aish.com/ho/p/48956731.html.

Chapter 7

1. Finis Jennings Dake, ed., *Dake's Annotated Reference Bible* (Lawrenceville, GA: Dake Publishing, 2014), 554.

2. Nosson Scherman, *The Rubin Edition of the Prophets: Samuel 1 and 2*, Art Scroll series (New York: Mesorah Publications, 2002), 11.

3. Ibid.,12.

4. Ibid.,10.

5. Tamar Kadari, "Hannah: Midrash and Aggadah," *Jewish Women: A Comprehensive Historical Encyclopedia*, Jewish Women's Archive, last modified March 20, 2009, http://jwa.org/encyclopedia/article/hannah-midrash-and-aggadah. ; Matthew Henry, *1 Peter, Matthew Henry Commentary on the Whole Bible (Complete)*, 1706, http://www.biblestudytools.com/commentaries/matthew-henry-complete/genesis/. ; Nosson Scherman, *The Rubin Edition of the Prophets: Samuel 1 and 2*, Art Scroll series (New York: Mesorah Publications, 2002), 13.

6. James S. Hewett, ed., "Illustrations Unlimited," *Pulpit Helps*, http://www.pulpithelps.com/www/resources/4.

7. Arie Uittenbogaard, "The Meaning of Miriam," *Abarim Publications*, http://www.abarim-publications.com/Meaning/Miriam.html#.WAYjGDKZODU.

8. Nosson Scherman, *The Artscroll English Tanach*, The Jewish Scriptures (New York: Mesorah Publishers, 2011), 1232.

9. *The Jerusalem Talmud*, Sanhedrin 69b and Sotah 11b (London: Williams and Norgate, 1886).

10. Tamar Kadari, "Daughter of Pharaoh: Midrash and Aggadah," *Jewish Women: A Comprehensive Historical Encyclopedia*, Jewish Women's Archive,

last modified March 1, 2009, http://jwa.org/encyclopedia/article/daughter
-of-pharaoh-midrash-and-aggadah.

11. Finis Jennings Dake, ed., *Dake's Annotated Reference Bible* (Lawrenceville, GA: Dake Publishing, 2014), 106.

12. Dina Coopersmith, "Women in the Bible #6: Miriam," *AISH.com*, last modified August 25, 2012, http://www.aish.com/jl/b/women/Women-in-the-Bible-6-Miriam.html.

13. Arie Uittenbogaard, "The Meaning of Mary," *Abarim Publications*, http://www.abarim-publications.com/Meaning/Mary.html#.WAYlzjKZODU.

14. Matthew 12:46; 13:55; Mark 6:3; John 2:12; Acts 1:14; 1 Corinthians 9:5; Galatians 1:19.

15. Spiros Zodhiates, *The Song of the Virgin* (Chattanooga, TN: AMG Publishers, 1974).

16. Derived from Genesis 50:1–14; *Shiva*, as it relates to Jewish bereavement practices, is the seven-day mourning period for the immediate family of the deceased.

17. The doctrine that the Bible is without error or fault in all its writings and teachings.

18. Robert McAnally Adams, "Week 2. Unto Generations: the Magnificat of Mary," *The Quotations Bible Study*, 2009, http://www.cqod.com/QBS/QBS12.pdf.

19. James S. Hewett, ed., "Illustrations Unlimited," Pulpit Helps, 187.

Chapter 8

1. Nosson Scherman, *The Rubin Edition of the Prophets: Samuel 1 and 2*, Art Scroll series (New York: Mesorah Publications, 2002), 19.

2. *The Babylonian Talmud*, Zevachim 17:B (Boston: New Talmud Publishing Company, 1903).

3. Nosson Scherman, *The Rubin Edition of the Prophets: Samuel 1 and 2*, Art Scroll series (New York: Mesorah Publications, 2002), 19.

4. Rev. H.D.M. Spence and Joseph S Exell, eds., "The First Book of Samuel," *The Pulpit Commentary*, vol. 9 (Peabody, MA: Hendrickson Publishers, 1985), 40.

5. Nosson Scherman, *The Rubin Edition of the Prophets: Samuel 1 and 2*, Art Scroll series (New York: Mesorah Publications, 2002), 19.

6. "The Seven Blessings," *InterFaithFamily*, http://www.interfaithfamily.com/life_cycle/weddings/The_Seven_Blessings.shtml.

7. Ibid.

8. Ibid.

9. Finis Jennings Dake, ed., *Dake's Annotated Reference Bible* (Lawrenceville, GA: Dake Publishing, 2014), 555.

10. Nosson Scherman, *The Rubin Edition of the Prophets: Samuel 1 and 2*, Art Scroll series (New York: Mesorah Publications, 2002), 21.

11. Adapted from C. H. Spurgeon, "Blessed in Him," (Sermon No. 2451, Metropolitan Tabernacle, February 7, 1886).

12. Ibid.

13. Lois Tyerberg, "Shema: To Hear is to Obey," *Our Rabbi Jesus*, last modified February 6, 2013, http://ourrabbijesus.com/articles/shema-to-hear-is-to -obey/.

14. Adapted from "Old Testament Studies: Lesson 7," *Torah Class: Rediscoveries of the Old Testament*, http://torahclass.com/old-testament-studies/1839-old -testament-survey/1916-lesson-7-old-testament-survey.

15. *The Jerusalem Talmud*, Sanhedrin 91b (London: Williams and Norgate, 1886).

16. Rev. H.D.M. Spence and Joseph S Exell, eds., "The First Book of Samuel," *The Pulpit Commentary*, vol. 9 (Peabody, MA: Hendrickson Publishers, 1985), 24.

Chapter 9

1. Nosson Scherman, *The Rubin Edition of the Prophets: Samuel 1 and 2*, Art Scroll series (New York: Mesorah Publications, 2002), 25.

2. Ibid., 29.

3. Ibid., 59.

4. Clovis G. Chappell, "1 Samuel: An Old-Time Mother," (Sermon, Pitts Theology Library, Emory University, Digital Collections), http://www.pitts .emory.edu/collections/digitalcollections/mss365.cfm.

5. Rev. H.D.M. Spence and Joseph S Exell, eds., "The First Book of Samuel," *The Pulpit Commentary*, vol. 9 (Peabody, MA: Hendrickson Publishers, 1985), 77.

6. Ibid., 88.

7. Emil G. Hirsch, Wilhelm Bacher, Jacob Zallel Lauterbach, eds., "Samuel," *Jewish Encyclopedia*, http://www.jewishencyclopedia.com/articles/13079 -samuel.

8. Ira M. Price, "The Schools of the Sons of the Prophets," *The Old Testament Student* (University of Chicago Press) 8, no. 7 (March 1889): 244-245.

9. Anne Adams, "Susanna Wesley: Mother of Methodism," *History's Women*, http://www.historyswomen.com/womenoffaith/SusannahWesley.html.

10. Ibid.

11. Sandy Dengler, *Susanna Wesley: Servant of God* (Chicago: Moody Publishers, 1987).

12. Arthur Dicken Thomas, Jr., "Profiles in Faith: Susanna Wesley (1669–1742)," *Knowing & Doing* (C. S. Lewis Institute), (Winter 2003), http://www. cslewisinstitute.org/webfm_send/499.

13. Milton V. Backman, Jr., "The Holiness-Pentecostal Movement," *Christian Churches of America* (Upper Saddle River, NJ: Pearson, 1983), PDF retrieved 21 March 2014, http://emp.byui.edu/marrottr/352folder /backmpentacostal.pdf.

14. *Christianity Today*, "John Wesley: Did You Know?," *Christianity Today*, 1983, http://www.christianitytoday.com/history/issues/issue-2/john-wesley-did-you-know.html.

15. Elesha Coffman, "The Wesleys: Founders of Methodism," *Christian History* 69 (2001), http://www.christianitytoday.com/history/issues/issue-69/.

Chapter 10

1. Adapted from J. Vernon McGee, *Through the Bible*, vol. 2 (Nashville, TN: Thomas Nelson, 1994), 125.

2. Ibid.

3. Ibid.

4. Adapted from Moshe Kempinski, "To Truly Sing," *Arutz Sheva: Israelnationalnews.com*, last modified January 2, 2012, http://www.israelnationalnews.com/Articles/Article.aspx/11213.

5. Ibid.

ABOUT THE AUTHOR

Diana Hagee is the wife of Pastor John Hagee, founder and senior pastor of Cornerstone Church in San Antonio, Texas. Diana leads the Women's Ministries at Cornerstone Church and coordinates all special events for John Hagee Ministries, Cornerstone Church, and Christians United for Israel. She is the author of *The King's Daughter*; *Ruth: The Romance of Redemption*; *Proclamations: Releasing the Power of God's Word*; *What Every Woman Wants in a Man*; and the *Not by Bread Alone Cookbook*. Pastor Hagee and Diana have five children and thirteen grandchildren.